Achieve Your Organization's Strategic Plan

Create a Right-Minded Team Management System
to Ensure All Teams Work as One

By
Dan Hogan
Certified Master Facilitator

Books by Dan Hogan

Reason, Ego, & the Right-Minded Teamwork Myth: The Philosophy and Process for Creating a Right-Minded Team That Works Together as One

Right-Minded Teamwork in Any Team: The Ultimate Team Building Method to Create a Team That Works as One

How to Facilitate Team Work Agreements: A Practical, 10-Step Process for Building a Right-Minded Team That Works as One

How to Apply the Right Choice Model: Create a Right-Minded Team That Works as One

7 Mindfulness Training Lessons: Improve Teammates' Ability to Work as One with Right-Minded Thinking

Right-Minded Teamwork: 9 Right Choices for Building a Team That Works as One

Design a Right-Minded, Team-Building Workshop: 12 Steps to Create a Team That Works as One

Achieve Your Organization's Strategic Plan: Create a Right-Minded Team Management System to Ensure All Teams Work as One

Copyright © 2022 by Dan Hogan
Publisher: Lord & Hogan LLC.
Contact Dan Hogan, Publisher, at Dan.Hogan@RightMindedTeamwork.com.
All rights reserved worldwide.

Visit RightMindedTeamwork.com to order additional books and other materials.

ISBN: 978-1-939585-13-4

Acknowledgments & Appreciations

To the thousands of teammates, team leaders,
and team-building facilitators with whom I've
worked with over the last 40 years,

Thank You

for being my teacher.

Collectively, we created this
awesome team-building program.

*Right-Minded Teamwork is a business-oriented,
psychological approach to team building where
acceptance, forgiveness, and adjustment
are teammate characteristics,
and customer satisfaction
is the team's result.*

In addition, there are several special people I want to joyfully acknowledge and thank for their contributions.

First and foremost, I want to convey my deep and heartfelt gratitude to our editor, Erin Leigh. Thanks to her superb editing and vital guidance, Right-Minded Teamwork is now much easier to understand and successfully integrate in your team. Thank you, Erin. The RMT book series would not have happened without you.
(To contact Erin, email erin@thechoice.life.)

Next, a giant thank you to the Ebook Launch team. Dane Low, our book cover designer, created exceptional cover designs for the Right-Minded Teamwork book series. Thank you for elevating Right-Minded Teamwork. (To reach Dane visit EbookLaunch.com.)

Another sincere thank you goes out to Cathi Bosco, our graphic artist, who renovated and modernized many of our Right-Minded Teamwork process models, graphics, and illustrations
(reach her at CathiBosco.com).
And I also want to thank the Media A-Team, who created the original and current versions of the Right Choice Model
(find them at Mediaateam.com).

Finally, I want to express my gratitude to Jackie D'Elia, our website and UX designer, who successfully modernized the RightMindedTeamwork.com website into an easy-to-use platform. Her work allows us to share the RMT books, models, and other resources and materials with the world. Thank you, Jackie.
(Contact Jackie at JackieDElia.com.)

CONTENTS

Preface

Welcome to Right-Minded Teamwork (RMT).

It is an honor to introduce you to this unique, real-world, continuous improvement teamwork method that has improved the lives and teams of thousands of people worldwide.

Apply this process in your teams, and you, too, will reap its benefits.

Apply this team-building method as your organization's *Team Management System,* and you will ensure all your teams are *working together as one* to achieve your organization's strategic plan.

Before we get started, let me answer a few questions that may be on your mind.

. . . . .

What Is Right-Minded Teamwork?

Right-Minded Teamwork is a business-oriented, psychological approach to team building where acceptance, forgiveness, and adjustment are teammate characteristics, and 100% customer satisfaction is the team's result.

What Is a Team Management System (TMS)?

An enterprise's Team Management System aligns all teammate goals, attitudes, and work behaviors, ensuring everyone is on the same page and doing their part to achieve the enterprise's vision, mission, and strategic goals.

How Does a TMS Work?

Your TMS is much like your employee performance management system, just on a team level.

Instead of individual performance evaluations, every team in the enterprise sets performance goals that are aligned with the enterprise's strategic plan. Every quarter, teams measure and report their actual results, and they set new goals for the next calendar quarter.

Undoubtedly, you have internal human resource management support to guide team leaders in effectively administering individual employee performance management reviews. Your TMS Steering Team will serve and support similarly. You will develop a team of Right-Minded Teamwork facilitators who will work directly with your team leaders and teammates to help them achieve their team goals and the organization's strategic plan.

What Are the Benefits?

Every team in the enterprise operates with clarity and focus. The enterprise consistently achieves a higher percentage of its strategic goals year over year.

How Long Does It Take to Reap the Benefits?

Within the first six to 12 months, your TMS will not only begin paying for itself, but you will also see evidence of organizational performance improvement. Within 18 to 24 months, your TMS will demonstrate and report consistent, enterprise-wide results.

Who Participates?

- Executive Leadership Team
- TMS Steering Team
- Internal (possibly external) team-building facilitators
- All teams will eventually participate

What Is This Book About?

In these pages, you will learn a strategic planning process for deploying the 5 Element, continuous improvement, Right-Minded Teamwork process throughout your organization.

Once you understand each Element of RMT, it will be clear how integrating Right-Minded Teamwork into your TMS will benefit you, your team, your entire organization, and your customers.

In this book, you will learn about the four phases of establishing a Team Management System and how to deploy them in your organization. After the final phase, you will establish your TMS as a permanent department.

As we explore these concepts together, you will find that Right-Minded Teamwork is practical. It produces positive business results by getting real work done. And above all, it naturally motivates teammates to grow.

The Right-Minded Teamwork Philosophy

The Right-Minded philosophy is founded on two universal truths:

None of us is as smart as all of us.

Right-Minded Teammates know that working collaboratively together, in a Right-Minded manner, is the only way to create the kind of teamwork that achieves and sustains 100% customer satisfaction.

Do no harm, and work as one.

As a Right-Minded Teammate, you can be firm, direct, gentle, and compassionate, all at the same time. You do not blame yourself or others for mistakes; you find and implement solutions. You and your teammates are allies, not adversaries. You work together towards your shared goals.

Why Right-Minded Teamwork?

There are many common "team-building" practices out there such as education, team games, and social events.

None of these are real-world methods. Not one of them produces proven, reliable results. If you have participated in them, you know what I mean.

(For more on why such exercises are not unique or dependable, go to RightMindedTeamwork.com, and search for the article, *"10 Worst Team Building Exercises."*)

Still, many well-meaning leaders continue using these tactics, trying to make them work. Usually, this is because they do not realize there is a better way: Right-Minded Teamwork.

A Real-World, Team-Building Method

A real-world approach to team building is the better way because it addresses and resolves real team issues. It is also the most reliable way to achieve and sustain high-performance teamwork.

Right-Minded Teamwork is a real-world, team-building process.

Applied intentionally, it has the power to transform your teams and your organization, bringing you all together to work as one and allowing you to achieve - or even exceed! - your organization's strategic goals.

Do You Want Your Teams to Work as One?

If you want to achieve unified teamwork, what processes and systems are you currently applying to get you there?

Now is the right time to create and deploy your Team Management System. Doing so improves your organization's chances of achieving its goals and strategic plan.

The Special Function of Executive Leaders

As a member of your organization's executive leadership team, you are responsible for leading, mentoring, and developing your leaders and employees.

Along with that responsibility, you have a special TMS function: *team transformation.*

Team transformation occurs when you:
- strengthen your individual Right-Minded Thinking
- strengthen your Executive Team's Right-Minded Thinking
- show all your leaders and employees, by your example, how to do the same.

How do you strengthen individual and collective Right-Minded Thinking?

Among other things, you actively live and demonstrate the Right-Minded Teamwork attitudes and behaviors presented later on in this book. You offer team-building support, and you provide your team members with RMT resources like the 5 Element Framework, the Right Choice Model, and team Work Agreements. No matter what organization you work for or where you are in the world, these RMT tools are available to you; there are no licensing or certification requirements.

The only request as you use these RMT tools is that you wholeheartedly accept your special function as a team transformer. Honoring your role will help your teams create and sustain Right-Minded Teamwork, which will significantly increase the likelihood of achieving your organization's strategic plan.

My Special Support Function

After my 35 years of active team-building facilitation, I am convinced that RMT is right for everyone, everywhere, forever. I know beyond a shadow of a doubt that RMT's TMS process *will* help make your organization, and the world you serve, a better place.

First, though, your teams need *you* to show them the Right-Minded Teamwork way.

As the author of this book and the RMT model, I have a special role to play in your journey to Right-Minded Teamwork. Though I have retired from active facilitation work, I am here to support you, if you desire it. If you offer RMT to your organization's teams, and you come across questions or challenges, reach out to me. Let me get to know you. Let me support your Right-Minded efforts. Together, we can create a Right-Minded world.

RMT Is for Everyone, Everywhere, Forever

In my years of facilitating teams around the globe, I have seen and experienced Right-Minded Teamwork firsthand countless times. RMT has proven itself as an intelligent and empowering teamwork system that *creates teams that work together as* ***one***.

Apply RMT, and you will improve your organization's work processes and strengthen relationships. Apply RMT, and your organization's teams will achieve 100% customer satisfaction and accomplish your strategic plan. Create and apply your Right-Minded Teamwork Team Management System, and you become an organization whose *teams work together as* ***one***.

Apply RMT, and *you* ***make the world a better place*** *for everyone, everywhere, forever.*

Let's get started right now.

Dan Hogan

TMS: An Overview

An enterprise's Team Management System (TMS) aligns the entire organization's goals, attitudes, and work behavior. An effective TMS ensures everyone is doing their part to achieve the enterprise's vision, mission, and strategic goals by improving their ability to work together as one.

There are four phases to creating and deploying your organization's customized TMS. Eventually, your TMS will apply Right-Minded Teamwork in every team in your enterprise. The four phases are deployed in this order:

Phase 1:
Executive Leadership Team applies RMT and launches the TMS.

Phase 2:
Steering Team creates, organizes, and pilots the TMS in a few teams.

Phase 3:
Steering Team measures performance and rolls out the TMS to the second group of teams.

Phase 4:
TMS is rolled out to all teams, and a permanent TMS department is established.

How RMT's Team Management System Works

TMS is much like your employee performance management system, just on a team level.

Instead of individual performance evaluations, every team in the enterprise sets performance goals that are aligned with your strategic plan. Teams measure and report their actual results every quarter, and they set new goals for the next 90 days.

You likely have internal human resource management support already in place to guide team leaders in effectively administering individual employee performance management reviews. The equivalent within your TMS will be a TMS Steering Team with at least four sub-teams to provide similar support for your program. We will introduce those teams in *TMS: A Detailed Explanation*, below, but of your four TMS Steering Team sub-teams, one will be your *RMT Facilitator Team*. Here, you will develop a group of RMT facilitators who will work directly with your team leaders and teammates to help them achieve their teamwork goals.

The following three teams will be initially involved in establishing the organization's TMS:
- Executive Leadership Team
- TMS Steering Team
- Internal (or possibly external) team-building facilitators

Eventually, the TMS will be rolled out across the organization, and all teams will participate.

Now, before we dive deeper into the process, let's take a brief, high-level look at what happens in each of the four phases of applying your TMS.

How to Apply a Team Management System

Phase 1:
Executive Leadership Team
Applies RMT & Launches TMS

- The enterprise adopts RMT as the standard teamwork process.
- The Executive Team implements RMT in its team.
- Executives establish a Steering Team that will start up and initially manage the TMS for the first two years.
- Phase duration: one to two months.

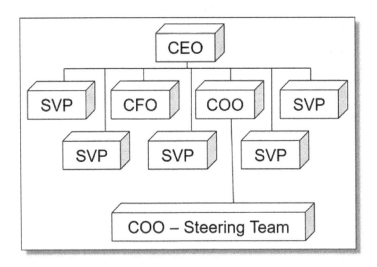

Phase 2:
Steering Team Creates, Organizes, & Pilots TMS 1.0

- The Steering Team creates the enterprise's startup TMS 1.0.
- Select individual teammates are chosen to become Right-Minded Teamwork team-building facilitators, or external facilitators are identified.
- The Steering Team and facilitators pilot the startup TMS 1.0 in two or three teams.
- After the pilot, in preparation for the second group of teams, the Steering Team fine-tunes the program into the TMS 2.0 plan.
- Using the Right-Minded Teamwork method, the Steering Team continues to manage the TMS towards Phase 4, where the TMS is rolled out throughout the organization and all teams are participating.
- Phase duration: four to six months.

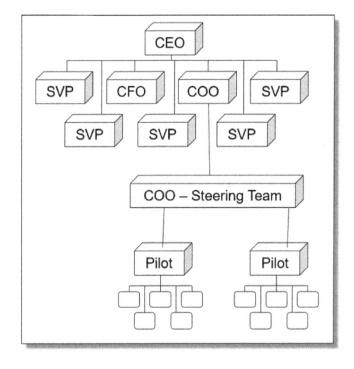

Phase 3:
Steering Team Measures Performance & Rolls Out TMS 2.0 to the Second Group of Teams

- After the pilot teams complete their first 90-day implementation plan, the first quarterly TMS results are reported.
- The TMS 2.0 is rolled out to the second round of five to 10 teams during the next 12 months.
- Within 24 months of the pilot, TMS quarterly reports demonstrate beneficial enterprise results.
- Results are communicated internally and externally.
- Phase duration: six to 12 months.

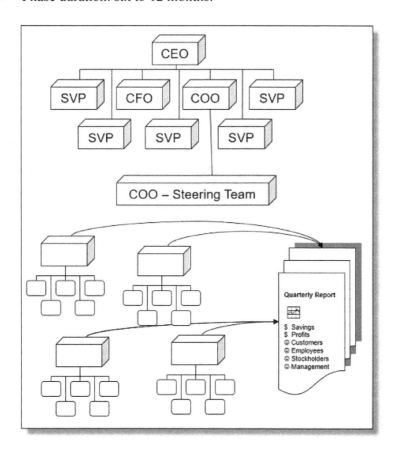

Phase 4:
Roll Out TMS to All Teams;
Establish a Permanent TMS Department

- The Steering Team is transformed into a stable growth and management phase with the Executive Team's support and guidance. Some original members are transferred to new opportunities, while other new members are chosen to lead and manage the TMS department.
- New reporting and governance structures are established.
- The new TMS leadership team uses RMT's continuous improvement approach to manage the TMS department going forward.
- The Steering Team begins a consistent and controlled TMS rollout to all teams.
- Phase duration: about six months to establish a permanent TMS department; indefinite continued usage of the TMS and RMT

By the time your organization has reached Phase 4, the TMS will have proven itself. Because the TMS program has succeeded in its first two years of operation, it now becomes a permanent program with leadership, staff, governance, and a budget.

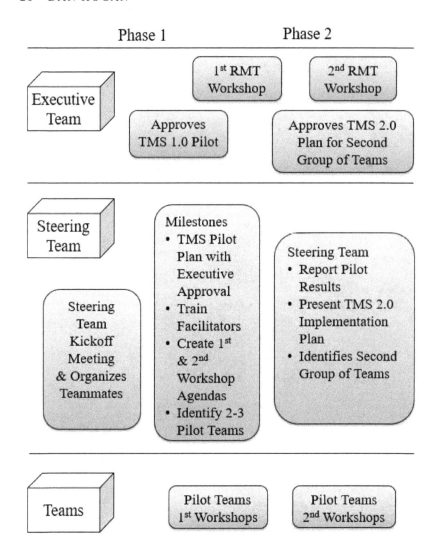

Phase 1   Phase 2

Executive Team

1st RMT Workshop

2nd RMT Workshop

Approves TMS 1.0 Pilot

Approves TMS 2.0 Plan for Second Group of Teams

Steering Team

Milestones
- TMS Pilot Plan with Executive Approval
- Train Facilitators
- Create 1st & 2nd Workshop Agendas
- Identify 2-3 Pilot Teams

Steering Team Kickoff Meeting & Organizes Teammates

Steering Team
- Report Pilot Results
- Present TMS 2.0 Implementation Plan
- Identifies Second Group of Teams

Teams

Pilot Teams 1st Workshops

Pilot Teams 2nd Workshops

	Phase 3	Phase 4

Executive Team

3rd RMT Workshop	Ongoing 90-Day Workshops

Approves TMS as a permanent department

Steering Team

TMS Milestones
- Fine-Tune TMS 2.0 program content
- Conduct facilitator training
- Tracks TMS team's performance and prepares ROI

Steering Team
- Quarterly Reports TMS Results
- Continue to roll out TMS to all teams

Teams

Pilot Teams 3rd Workshops	Pilot Teams Ongoing 90-Day Workshops

Second Group of Teams 1st Workshops	Second Group of Teams 2nd Workshops

Rollout TMS to All Teams

TMS: A Detailed Explanation

Phase 1:
Executive Leadership Team
Applies RMT & Launches TMS

Organizational Tasks

1. Select one executive to sponsor, launch, and lead the TMS for the first two years. Also, choose six to 12 key employees from all parts of the enterprise to serve on the Steering Team for the first year. Choose a Steering Team Leader from among those employees.

   It's best if your Steering Team members work full-time to create and deploy your TMS, especially the team leader and sub-team leaders.

2. Establish a TMS vision, success criteria, and financial goals. Authorize the Steering Team to be accountable for achieving those goals.

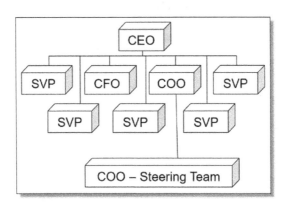

3. Announce the TMS's vision: *The Team Management System's vision is to ensure all our teams are working together as one to achieve our organization's business goals and strategic plan.*

4. Identify and select employees to be trained as your organization's Right-Minded team-building facilitators and trainers.

5. Agree on a "go slow to go fast" philosophy. Agree that the TMS is a top-down rollout, which means senior executives and leaders will improve their teamwork first, and then, over time, all teams will be asked to do the same.

   This means it might take several years to roll out the TMS program to every team in the organization.

Duration: Phase 1 will last one to two months and will include at least one executive team-building workshop and the formation of your TMS Steering Team.

Executive Leadership

1. Administer an executive teamwork assessment to determine strengths and weaknesses within the Executive Team's tactical performance and human interaction performance.

    There are numerous assessments your executive team can administer, including RMT's Team Performance Factor Assessment. You will find this assessment in the *5 Elements: Right-Minded Teamwork in Any Team* section later in this book, after the four Phases. The *Team Performance Factor Assessment* can be found inside *Element #4 – Team Operating System.*

2. During Phases 1 and 2, the Executive Team completes its first two team-building workshops. All TMS teams, including the Executive Team, will, from now on, conduct team workshops every 90 days. A team's first two or three workshops typically last six to eight hours. But after the third or fourth workshop, the quarterly workshops will become shorter and last only a few hours.

    Remember: The Executive Team should lead by example and be a role model for creating Right-Minded Teamwork.

3. The Executive Team schedules the next three quarterly meetings to improve their leadership performance and support the TMS Steering Team in rolling out the program.

Steering Team

1. The senior executive TMS sponsor forms the TMS Steering Team and agrees to stay with the team for two years. Afterward, the Executive Team will determine this team's governance and reporting structure.

2. The Steering Team is formed with members who will serve on the team for one to two years. After the first year, new team members will join. Eventually, 50% of members will roll off each year, making way for new team members.

3. The TMS sponsor and the Steering Team Leader organize and form the Steering Team and lead the kickoff meeting. See below: *Steering Team Formation: A High-Level, 90-Day Plan.*

Leadership Teams

1. Along with the senior executive TMS sponsor, the Steering Team Leader announces the TMS program to the next level of leadership.

2. Those leaders ask questions and offer suggestions for creating and implementing a successful startup TMS process and pilot.

Phase 2:
Steering Team Creates, Organizes, & Pilots TMS 1.0

Executive Leadership

1. While the Executive Team is improving its teamwork, the Steering Team takes four to eight weeks to finalize the startup TMS design and rollout strategy plan.

   In this phase, the Steering Team presents the recommended startup design and strategy to the Executive Team for discussion, modification, and eventual approval.

Steering Team

1. With the executive sponsor's support, the Steering Team conducts several team meetings to apply the appropriate Right-Minded Teamwork Elements from RMT's 5 Elements Model to their team. Doing so ensures all teammates function efficiently and effectively.

2. Essential RMT Elements to integrate include:

   a. Business Goals (RMT Element #1) focused specifically on achieving a successful TMS program

   b. Work Agreements (RMT Element #3)

   c. Team Operating System (RMT Element #4) *(See below for details on Forming the Steering Team: A High-Level, 90-Day Plan.)*

3. With guidance from the executives and possible external consultation, the Steering Team creates a startup TMS design complete with timelines, cost/benefit budgeting analysis, and expected business outcomes for employees, the organization, customers, and financial markets.

4. The team schedules and announces the TMS program further down in the leadership chain of command.

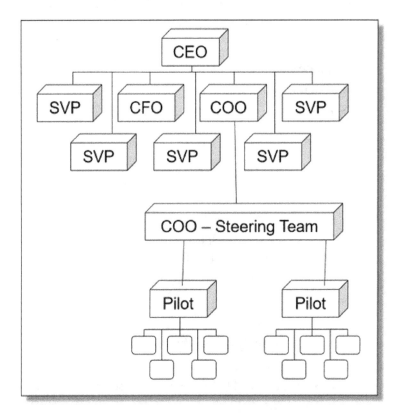

5. After receiving feedback from other leaders as to how to improve the TMS, the Steering Team creates a detailed startup pilot program and rollout plan. They present the plan to the Executive Team for modification and final approval.

Note: It is possible the TMS Steering Team will want to change the *Team Management System* program name. You certainly have Right-Minded Teamwork's permission to do so. It can be most effective to make a name change at the beginning of Phase 4 when your organization transforms the TMS into a permanent department.

6. Once approved, the team schedules and announces the TMS program to the rest of the organization.

7. The Steering Team establishes the following four sub-teams, and each sub-team chooses a leader.

   • The *TMS Liaison Team* is the primary point of contact between the Executive Team, the Steering Team, and the entire organization. The Steering Team Leader leads this sub-team.

   • The *RMT Facilitator Assignment Team* is the clearinghouse for receiving team-building support requests.

   • The *RMT Facilitator Training Team* identifies and trains facilitators.

   • The *RMT Implementation Design Team* builds the organization's standard, team-building process.

8. One or two Steering Team members are assigned to monitor and track each pilot team to ensure the Phase 2 startup process goes smoothly. They monitor and track each TMS team's business plan to ensure horizontal, vertical, and integrated alignment with the company's strategic goals, watching out for duplicated efforts or competing improvement initiatives.

   A Steering Team member will also be assigned to monitor and track all Phase 3 teams. Monitoring can stop in Phase 4.

9. As the point of contact between the Executive Team, the Steering Team, and the entire organization, the *TMS Liaison Team*:

   - Identifies and notifies the teams who will participate in the pilot (Phase 2) and the second round (Phase 3). RMT recommends no more than three teams participate in the three-month pilot and that between five and 10 teams participate in the second round.
   - Collects quarterly performance data and compiles the information into the organization's TMS quarterly Report of Improvement.
   - Presents the report to the Executive Team and then communicates the result to the organization.

   The goals of the TMS Liaison Team are to ensure effective TMS communication with stakeholders and help promote genuine excitement and support for the TMS.

10. The ***RMT Facilitator Training Team*** identifies and trains facilitators in RMT's 12 Steps workshop design process plus RMT's 5 Elements Model and Implementation Plan. This team exists to create and teach basic, intermediate, and advanced facilitator training classes.

Depending on the size of your organization and your TMS needs, you could have between six and 20 internal facilitators. RMT recommends full-time facilitators, but you could include part-time or even external facilitators.

This sub-team teaches the first basic facilitator training early in Phase 2. They also schedule future first-time facilitation classes in Phase 3 and 4. In Phase 3, the team develops intermediate and advanced facilitator training classes and begins teaching them in Phase 4.

Facilitators learn how to implement and facilitate the following methods, presented later in this book:
- 5 Elements of Right-Minded Teamwork
- RMT's three-workshop, 90-day Implementation Plan
- Team Work Agreements
- 12 Steps to Design an RMT Workshop

The RMT Facilitator Training Team ensures RMT facilitators are effective in helping their teams achieve Right-Minded Teamwork and the organization's TMS goals.

11. The **RMT Facilitator Assignment Team** is the clearinghouse for receiving team-building support requests. This team ensures they are familiar with all RMT facilitators' skills, abilities, capabilities, and availability. Their goal is to create good matches between team needs and facilitator skills to encourage Right-Minded Teamwork.

    For the Executive Team specifically, the Steering Team Leader, the Executive TMS sponsor, and the CEO discuss and agree on who will be their facilitator. They may choose anyone within the organization or outside of it.

12. The **RMT Implementation Design Team** is responsible for building your organization's standard, team-building process. Using the 5 Elements of Right-Minded Teamwork and the 90-day Implementation Plan, this team creates the following team-building agendas:

    - TMS orientation meeting for enrolling a new team
    - Agendas for the first three workshops in the TMS process

    All teams and RMT facilitators adapt these agendas to fit their specific team needs.

    Once the organization reaches Phase 4, the RMT Implementation Design Team will also create a final team-building agenda that teams can adapt and continue to use for their quarterly team-building workshops.

    This team has achieved its goals when all TMS teams and RMT facilitators have the teamwork tools and support they need to create Right-Minded Teamwork and achieve the organization's TMS goals.

Agenda Templates: This book contains five workshop agenda templates that you may adopt and adapt to meet your team's needs and TMS goals. These templates can be found in the *RMT Implementation Design & Facilitator Training* section. You may also download these templates by accessing this book's companion, **Reusable Resources & Templates**, available at RightMindedTeamwork.com. Learn more in the Resources section of this book.

13. The **RMT Implementation Design Team** is also responsible for integrating existing HR initiatives and training programs, like individual performance management, leadership, and diversity training, into the TMS.

14. During Phase 2, each pilot team participates in at least two team-building workshops where they establish business goals, Work Agreements, and a Team Operating System. With their facilitator's help, they follow RMT's *90-Day Implementation Plan*, found below, which includes three workshops and a 90-day operating system.

15. If any unexpected situations or issues arise during the pilot rollout, the Steering Team serves as the primary mediator and decision-maker for successfully addressing and resolving them.

16. Upon completing the startup and the pilot rollout, the Steering Team fine-tunes the program into the TMS 2.0 plan for broader enterprise deployment, focusing on the second group of teams to participate in TMS.

17. They present the revised TMS 2.0 plan to the Executive Team for modification and approval.

18. The Steering Team identifies and notifies the second group of teams that they will participate in TMS 2.0. Depending on your TMS capability, you might choose between five and 10 teams to participate in the second round.

Duration: Phase 2 will last four to six months. The primary goal is to complete a successful, 90-day pilot with the first round of teams.

Leadership Teams

1. Some leadership teams may participate in the TMS pilot launch, but every senior leadership team will eventually apply the TMS process, facilitated by a qualified, Right-Minded, team-building facilitator, within the first nine to 12 months of the program.

2. Upon participation, every leadership team creates a business plan in alignment with the company's strategic goals.

3. Plans should outline clear business goals and objectives for the team, map out a plan for meeting or exceeding those goals, and create Work Agreements that describe how teammates will work as one in an emotionally mature, proactive way. To do so, they use RMT's *90-Day Implementation Plan*, found below, which includes three workshops and a 90-day operating system.

All Other Teams

1. Eventually, all teams will participate in the Team Management System. But for now, only the teams participating in Phase 2 will create their business plan in alignment with the company's strategic goals.

2. As with leadership teams, other team plans should outline clear business goals and objectives for the team, map out a plan for meeting or exceeding those goals, and create Work Agreements that describe how teammates will work as one in an emotionally mature, proactive way. To do so, they use RMT's *90-Day Implementation Plan*, found below, which includes three workshops and a 90-day operating system.

Phase 3:
Steering Team Measures Performance & Rolls Out TMS 2.0 to the Second Group of Teams

Phase 3 begins when the second group of teams starts participating in the TMS. Between five and 10 teams participate in this second round.

By the start of this Phase, the Executive Team will have completed at least two team-building workshops, and the Steering Team will have presented the first TMS Quarterly Performance Report.

Executive Leadership

1. Executives receive the first TMS Quarterly Performance Report and TMS 2.0 improvement recommendations.

2. The Executive Team makes any necessary decisions and gives needed support to the TMS Steering Team.

3. The leaders discuss and agree on the specific organizational performance improvements presented in the quarterly scorecard report that they want to publish internally and externally.

Steering Team

1. From now on, the Steering Team presents a consolidated TMS Quarterly Performance Report to the Executive Team, including specific recommendations for ongoing organizational performance improvement.

2. After the first year, new members join the Steering Team.

   The eventual goal is to reach a 50% annual turnover. The Steering Team creates a plan to achieve that goal between year two and three.

3. The Steering Team identifies the third group of teams and notifies them of their upcoming participation in Phase 4.

   Every three months thereafter, new teams begin participating in the TMS program until all the organization's teams are enrolled.

Leadership Team

1. All leadership teams are held accountable for meeting or exceeding performance goals as well as tracking their own team's performance and that of their direct-report teams.

All Other Teams

1. Quarterly, all participating teams report their progress in the form of subjective and objective business outcomes.

    See the *5 Workshop Agendas* section below for a Report of Improvement Template.

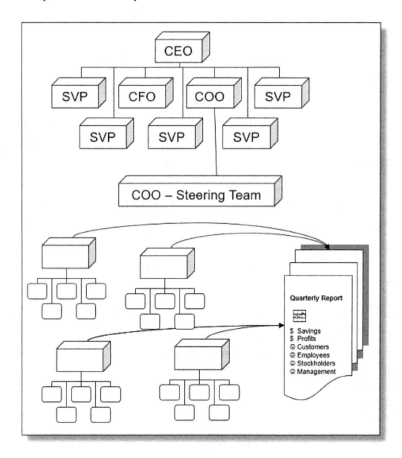

Phase 4:
Roll Out TMS to All Teams;
Establish a Permanent TMS Department

1. The Steering Team is transformed into a stable growth and management phase with the Executive Team's support and guidance.

2. Some original members are transferred to new opportunities, while other new members are chosen to lead and manage the TMS department.

3. New reporting and governance structures are established.

4. The new TMS leadership team uses RMT's continuous improvement *Team Operating System* to manage the TMS department going forward.

5. The Steering Team begins a consistent and controlled TMS rollout to all teams.

Duration: It will take about six months to establish a permanent TMS department. Because the TMS program has succeeded in its first two years of operation, it becomes a permanent program with leadership, staff, governance, and a budget.

. . . . .

Now that we've reviewed the four Phases of establishing your TMS, the remaining sections of this book will support all your TMS sub-teams in achieving your TMS goals.

Steering Team Formation:
A High-Level, 90-Day Plan

The following high-level plan will help you form your Team Management System's Steering Team. It describes the Steering Team's kickoff meeting and outlines actions and objectives to achieve in the first 90 days.

Before kicking off the team, the executive sponsor selects a Steering Team Leader. Both leaders provide lots of structure to Steering Team members, and both are more directive than collaborative in the beginning.

However, after 60 to 90 days, the Steering Team Leader moves into a more collaborative and consensus-building leadership style.

By the end of the first 90 days of operation, the Steering Team creates and begins following a Team Operating System that helps the team roll out the TMS program to the entire organization within 24 months. Steering Team members utilize Right-Minded Teamwork's *Team Operating System* for guidance.

During the kickoff, Steering Team members are encouraged to ask lots of questions, understand their job assignments, and agree to follow Right-Minded Teamwork behavior.

The Steering Team Leader, along with the TMS sponsor, organizes the team's formation using this 90-day plan as a guide. They create the team's start-up goals, operating structure, team member responsibilities, and performance expectations.

Please note: This 90-day timeline may be unrealistic or too aggressive for your TMS program. Your goal is to deploy these tasks in a timeline that is best for your organization. Remember the commitment you made in Phase 1 to adopt a "go slow to go fast" philosophy. It is worth taking the time now to create and secure a strong TMS foundation. Doing so will allow you to go faster in the future.

Day 1:
Steering Team Kickoff Meeting

Purpose: Formally sanction the TMS Steering Team established goals and assign startup job roles and responsibilities.

Attendees: All Steering Team members, Steering Team Leader, and the executive TMS sponsor

Outcomes:

1. Present the team's TMS business goals and startup team values.

2. Present and clarify the team's 90-day operating structure.

3. Create the four sub-teams within the Steering Team.

4. Clarify individual teammate roles and responsibilities.

5. Present specific performance expectations.

Agenda Topics:

1. Present the team's business goals and startup team values.

   a. Present and embrace the TMS Steering Team vision and mission, and understand how the team aligns with the enterprise's strategic goals.

   b. Present the team's first set of objectives. The primary aim is to create and implement a pilot program.

2. Present and clarify the team's startup operating structure.

    a. The leader presents a 90-day operating system that answers the TMS Steering Team *Operating Agreements* questions below and shares how the Steering Team will make decisions using *Decision-Making Work Agreements*. (We'll talk more about these in the upcoming section *5 Elements: Right-Minded Teamwork in Any Team*, when we *review Element #4: Team Operating System.*)

    b. The team arranges to meet once per week for at least the first 30 days and every two weeks thereafter for the first 60 to 90 days.

    c. By the end of the first 90 days, the team agrees to have created a *TMS Steering Team Charter* that the executive sponsor approves.

3. Create the Steering Team's four sub-teams, as previously described in the detailed explanation of Phase 2 of RMT's TMS rollout plan. Determine sub-team leaders and identify objectives.

- The **TMS Liaison Team** is the primary point of contact between the Executive Team, the Steering Team, and the entire organization. The Steering Team Leader leads this sub-team.
- The **RMT Facilitator Training Team** identifies and trains facilitators.
- The **RMT Facilitator Assignment Team** is the clearinghouse for receiving team-building support requests.
- The **RMT Implementation Design Team** builds the organization's standard team-building process.

4. Clarify individual teammate responsibilities.

    a. All teammates are assigned to a sub-team and given specific objectives, responsibilities, timelines, and milestones.

    b. Teammates accept that conflict or disagreements could happen, and if they do, they commit to resolving them.

5. Present specific performance expectations.

    a. The executive sponsor and the Steering Team Leader share their expectations for creating and sustaining productive working relationships. You can use the *Team Leader Expectations* list below to formulate your ideas.

    b. Teammates surface potential problems that might occur in the first 90 days. Additionally, teammates create Work Agreements to prevent or mitigate those challenges.

TMS Steering Team Operating Agreements

The executive TMS sponsor and Steering Team Leader provide teammates with answers to the following questions and topics.

1. Making key decisions:
    a. When will consensus be best?
    b. If we can't come to a team consensus, how will vital decisions be made?
    c. Who decides who decides?
    d. What kinds of decisions must teammates check with the leaders about first?

For more on team decision-making, keep an eye out for the upcoming section *5 Elements: Right-Minded Teamwork in Any Team,* specifically Element #4, where we'll talk about *Decision-Making Work Agreements* within your RMT Team Operating System.

2. Meeting management:
    a. What techniques will be standard for the team? Agendas, time allotments, breaks, starting and stopping on time, and use of process checks?

3. Follow-through on commitments:
    a. What can teammates expect from one another?
    b. How will competing priorities be resolved?

4. Behavior norms:
   a. What is okay to do or say?
   b. What is not okay?

5. Delivering bad news:
   a. How will feedback be given when things go wrong?
   b. What is a teammate's responsibility for sharing or withholding information that impacts team performance?
   c. How will tough news be given in a supportive way?

6. Conflicts or disagreements between teammates:
   a. Who should initiate a discussion about a perceived conflict? When? How?
   b. What about involving others who were not part of a conflict?
   c. When should assistance be requested?

7. Celebrating successes:
   a. What warrants a celebration?
   b. What kinds of celebrations make teammates feel rewarded and valued?

8. Roles and responsibilities:
   a. What are the expectations for the team leader and teammates?

Team Leader Expectations

The new TMS Steering Team Leader must share their expectations with the team. Sharing answers to some or all of the questions below will make it easier for teammates to interact with you and each other.

Present your answers in the first or second team meeting. Encourage teammates to continue asking clarifying questions.

1. What are the top three performance expectations or goals you have for your teammates and for the Steering Team?

2. What are your top three performance expectations for yourself?

3. How often do you want to see or talk to teammates?

4. When is something important enough to interrupt you in the office or to call you at home?

5. What works or does not work for you with your leadership or management style?

6. If a teammate thinks you are about to make a mistake, what is the best way for them to express it?

7. What is the best way for teammates to express disagreement with you?

8. What are your expectations for being kept informed?

9. What are your expectations of teammates and yourself when the team makes a mistake?

10. Do you have a temper? If so, what should teammates do or not do if you lose self-control?

11. What are your pet peeves? What makes you mad? What do you not want from your teammates?

Day 2 to 31:
Charter & Create Pilot

Once they are formed, each sub-team's tasks and projects occur simultaneously.

In the first month, the **TMS Liaison Team** will:
- Create a first draft Steering Team Charter (see example below).
- Create a first draft Team Operating System for the Steering Team that includes governance and budgeting for the first two years.
- Create the TMS pilot program.
- When the TMS 1.0 pilot program plans are finalized, the Steering Team presents the plan to the Executive Team for modification and approval. This occurs somewhere between Day 25 and 31.

The **RMT Facilitator Training Team** will:
- Immediately begin creating a Facilitator Training class for the first four to six facilitators.
- Conduct the class as soon as possible.
- Assign two facilitators per pilot team.

The **RMT Facilitator Assignment Team** will:
- Identify and notify two or three teams to participate in the TMS 1.0 pilot program.

The **RMT Implementation Design Team** will:
- Immediately begin creating the first two workshop agendas that the pilot teams and facilitators will use as guides. See Day 32 to 60 for details.

Day 32 to 60:
Launch TMS 1.0 Pilot

Launch your TMS 1.0 Pilot with a
Pilot Team Announcement & TMS Orientation Meeting.

All Steering Team members, participating pilot teams, and facilitators attend a TMS orientation meeting to learn about their TMS involvement. In the *5 Workshop Agendas for your RMT Implementation Plan* section, you will find a memo, *An Orientation: Introducing our Team Management System (TMS),* which you can adapt and send to teammates before the orientation.

In this meeting, participants learn about TMS and their role in ensuring its success. At the end of this meeting, the teams will break out and begin planning their first workshop.

When the TMS 2.0 is eventually rolled out to the second group of teams, the team leader and team facilitator will conduct a similar orientation just for their team.

Here are some important topics to share in your TMS orientation.

- The Team Management System is a new and ongoing program designed to help the organization achieve its strategic plan. Teammates will not only improve their ability to "work together as one," they will commit to do their part to achieve the organization's vision, mission, and strategic goals.

- Since the TMS is new, the Executive and Steering Teams have agreed to pilot and test the program before rolling it out to the entire organization. Pilot participation is vitally important because it helps improve the program, which ensures it succeeds.

- All teams will eventually participate, and every team, with the support of a team facilitator, will conduct a team workshop every 90 days from now on. At first, workshops will be about six to eight hours long, but by the third workshop, they will be much shorter.

- Our TMS will follow the Right-Minded Teamwork process, and the Executive Team has already begun applying it in their team.

- This pilot will last 90 days. Your team will monitor, track, and report your actual performance. With the assistance of your two team co-facilitators and your assigned TMS Steering Team member, you will also offer improvement suggestions on how to improve the program into TMS 2.0.

- Eventually, all teams will report quarterly improvements data that will be compiled into an organizational Improvement Report.

- As soon as this pilot group completes its second team workshop, we will enroll a second group of five to 10 more teams in the TMS 2.0 program, where teams will work with one facilitator instead of two.

- Your team facilitators are trained and ready to support you. They have three workshop agendas to show you. You will use them as guides for your first three workshops. And, for your first workshop, you are asked to identify one or two teamwork topics you would like to address.

Then you officially launch your TMS by saying, *"So, for the next 30 to 60 minutes or so, let's break out into your respective teams and start discussing potential topics to address in your first team-building event. Your co-facilitators will help you, and you will also schedule the day and time for your first workshop."*

Also, during this second month, the **TMS Liaison Team** will:

1. Enhance the Steering Team Operating System
   a. Include short and long-term goals for the TMS program.
   b. Begin discussing how and where this team should permanently reside in the organization by the end of its second year of operation.

2. Attend Weekly / Bi-Weekly Steering Team Meetings
   a. After the first pilot team workshops, teammates discuss what they have learned and how to adjust and improve the TMS program.
   b. A group of new teams is identified and selected to participate in the second round of the TMS. Depending on the Steering Team's capability and available facilitators, RMT recommends selecting five to 10 teams for the second round.

3. Begin TMS 2.0
   a. Using any available early pilot feedback, continue improving the TMS program. The revamped version of the program is called TMS 2.0.
   b. Begin preparing to present the improved program to the Executive Team.

The **RMT Facilitator Training Team** will:

1. Complete the first Facilitator Basic Training
2. Assign new facilitators to pilot teams
3. Conduct the first team-building workshop for all pilot teams
4. Through the facilitating process, identify more people to be trained as team-building facilitators

The **RMT Facilitator Assignment Team** will:

1. Track the Pilot teams' progress
   a. Steering Team members who attend their pilot team's workshops offer support and learn how the TMS program can be improved for the second round of teams that will participate.

The **RMT Implementation Design Team** will:

1. Create the first three team-building workshop agendas
2. Test-drive the first agenda with all pilot teams in their first team-building workshop

A team's first workshop could be a six to eight-hour meeting, depending on their specific desired outcomes.

Typically in the team's first workshop, they create team Work Agreements (RMT Element #3) and maybe an improvement project that will successfully address their chosen topics. They also identify and commit to psychological goals and values (RMT Element #2) that describe their ideal work attitudes and behaviors.

Each team agrees on how to track their progress with the expressed hope they will show demonstrable results within 90 days. At least one Steering Team member is assigned to each team to support them and help them track.

Before the team closes its first workshop, they schedule their second workshop within two to four weeks. In their second workshop, the team reaffirms their business goals (RMT Element #1) and agrees on improving their Team Operating System (RMT Element #4).

At the end of the second workshop, they schedule their third workshop, which will focus on teammate growth and development (RMT Element #5). You will find more on the three-workshop approach in the upcoming section *5 Elements: RMT Implementation Plan.*

Agenda Templates: This book contains five workshop agenda templates that you may adopt and adapt to meet your team's needs and TMS goals. These templates can be found in the *RMT Implementation Design & Facilitator Training* section below. You may also download these templates by accessing this book's companion, ***Reusable Resources & Templates***, available at RightMindedTeamwork.com. Learn more in the Resources section of this book.

Day 61 to 90:
Create TMS 2.0

In the third month of your TMS program, the **TMS Liaison Team** will:

1. Develop a TMS 2.0 plan
   a. Even though the pilot teams have yet to complete their first 90 days in the TMS, at this point, the Steering Team has enough subjective and objective data to create a TMS 2.0 plan for the second group of participating teams.

2. Compile the first Enterprise Quarterly Performance Report
   a. With data on hand, the Steering Team creates its first report and prepares to present it to the Executive Team.
   b. The report includes lessons learned, best and worst practices, financial data, and subjective data gathered from the two to three pilot teams.
   c. Most importantly, it shows how these teams' actual results are helping the organization achieve its strategic goals.

3. Present the TMS 2.0 plan and Performance Report
   a. The Executive and Steering Teams discuss, modify, and agree on the TMS 2.0 program.
   b. The Steering Team prepares to launch TMS 2.0 with the second round of participating teams.

The **RMT Facilitator Training Team** will:

1. Continue to identify and train new facilitators
2. Begin to create an intermediate and advanced facilitator training class

The **RMT Facilitator Assignment Team** will:

1. Begin the process of matching the internal team-building needs of the second group of teams with qualified facilitators

The **RMT Implementation Design Team** will:

1. Continue to monitor and modify the first three workshop agendas

Day 90 & Beyond:
Launch TMS 2.0

After three months, the **TMS Liaison Team** will:

1. Shift to bi-weekly Steering Team meetings

   a. Steering Team members report participating team progress and offer TMS improvement suggestions.

   b. The Liaison Team identifies the third group of teams to enroll in the TMS program after the second group completes its first 90 days of the program.

   c. The Steering Team continues to use the RMT Operating System to improve its performance.

2. Compile the second TMS Enterprise Quarterly Performance Report

   a. When the second group completes its first 90 days, the Steering Team completes the second performance report. This report is more comprehensive than the first one.

   b. The team presents the second report to the Executive Team for review.

   c. The executives provide the team with guidance and support.

3. Continue to roll out the TMS to batches of teams, working down through the organization, until all teams are enrolled in the TMS

   a. Within 24 months, TMS quarterly reports demonstrate beneficial enterprise results.

   b. With the Executive Team's support and guidance, the Steering Team establishes reporting structures and a continuous improvement Team Operating System to manage the TMS from now on.

The **RMT Facilitator Training Team** will:

1. Continue to train new facilitators

2. Establish a Facilitator Sharing Network where facilitators learn best practices and new skills, and RMT content

The **RMT Facilitator Assignment Team** will:

1. Schedule the Team Announcement & TMS orientation for the second round of five to 10 teams.

   When the TMS 2.0 is rolled out to the second group of teams, the team leader and team facilitator may conduct a similar orientation just for their team. In the *5 Workshop Agendas for your RMT Implementation Plan* section, you will find a memo, *An Orientation: Introducing our Team Management System [TMS],* which leaders can adapt and send to teammates before the orientation.

   For the first team-building workshop, teammates are asked to identify one or two teamwork topics they would like to address. The team-building facilitator helps them prepare for the workshop.

Last but not least, the **RMT Implementation Design Team** will:

1. Continue to integrate and leverage current training programs with TMS

2. Link other HR initiatives to TMS, like individual performance management, leadership, and diversity

3. Create the fourth and final adaptable, 90-day agenda

Steering Team Charter

Here is a simple charter you can use as a template to create your own.

Purpose:
Create, launch, lead, and manage our Team Management System.

Vision:
Ensure all teams are working together as one and are doing their part to achieve the organization's strategic goals.

Mission:
Create and launch a TMS pilot, adjust the TMS after the pilot, continue rolling out to the organization, and finally transition the Steering Team into a permanent operating department.

Values:
Every employee contributes to achieving our strategic goals. We believe, support, and enable collaboration.

- We do no harm.
- We work as one.
- We believe none of us is as smart as all of us.

Members:
List names of teammates, the Steering Team Leader, and the executive sponsor

Steering Team Operating System:

We apply the RMT continuous improvement Team Operating System.

Our Steering Team includes four sub-teams.

The *TMS Liaison Team* is the primary point of contact between the Executive Team, the Steering Team, and the entire organization. This team is responsible for collecting all quarterly team performance results and compiling them into the Report of Improvement, then presenting them to the Executive Team and the entire organization.

The goals of the TMS Liaison Team are to ensure effective TMS communication with stakeholders and help promote genuine excitement and support for the TMS.

The *RMT Facilitator Training Team* identifies and trains facilitators in RMT's 12 Steps workshop design process plus RMT's 5 Elements Model and Implementation Plan. This team exists to create and teach basic, intermediate, and advanced facilitator training classes.

The *RMT Facilitator Training Team* ensures RMT facilitators are effective in helping their teams achieve Right-Minded Teamwork and the organization's TMS goals.

The *RMT Facilitator Assignment Team* is the clearinghouse for receiving team-building support requests. This team ensures they are familiar with all RMT facilitators' skills, abilities, capabilities, and availability.

Their goal is to create good matches between team needs and facilitator skills to encourage Right-Minded Teamwork.

The ***RMT Implementation Design Team*** is responsible for building your organization's standard, team-building process. Using the 5 Elements of Right-Minded Teamwork and the 5 Elements Implementation Plan, this team creates three team-building agendas, one for each of the team's first three workshops in the TMS process. All teams and RMT facilitators adapt these agendas to fit their specific team needs.

Once the organization reaches Phase 4, the RMT Implementation Design Team will also create a final team-building agenda that teams can adapt and continue to use for their quarterly team-building workshops. This team has achieved its goals when all TMS teams and RMT facilitators have the teamwork tools and support they need to create Right-Minded Teamwork and achieve the organization's TMS goals.

Steering Team Metrics:

The TMS 1.0 pilot program will be launched and completed within our first four months.

The second group of teams will participate in TMS 2.0 within the first six months.

All leadership teams will participate within the first nine to 12 months.

All teams will participate in TMS within the first 24 months.

Quarterly Performance Reports will clearly show our TMS program works and benefits our customers and ourselves.

The Steering Team will transition into a permanent operating department within two years.

RMT Implementation Design & Facilitator Training

The ***RMT Facilitator Training Team*** and ***RMT Implementation Design Team*** will use the following RMT processes to create a standard, team-building program and a facilitator training course.

- Reason, Ego & the Right-Minded Teamwork Myth
- 5 Elements: Right-Minded Teamwork in Any Team
- 5 Elements: RMT Implementation Plan
- 5 Workshop Agendas for your RMT Implementation Plan
- 10 Steps: How to Facilitate Team Work Agreements
- 12 Steps: Design a Right-Minded Team-Building Workshop
- 30 Right-Minded Teamwork Attitudes & Behaviors
- What Is the Right Choice Model?

Let's take a brief look at each of these RMT concepts now.

RMT Facilitator Training Team

At first, the *RMT Facilitator Training Team* will create a basic facilitation class that instructs participants in the methods presented below. Then, at the beginning of Phase 3, this sub-team will develop and teach an intermediate and advanced facilitator class.

Supplemental Facilitator Training & External Facilitators

There are many excellent facilitator training programs that you may choose to use in your TMS. The International Institute for Facilitation is a valuable resource where you will find Certified Master Facilitators and other facilitation training materials. Their website is INIFAC.org.

RMT Implementation Design Team

The *Implementation Design Team* will use 5 Elements of Right-Minded Teamwork and the 5 Elements Implementation Plan to create three team-building agendas for each of the team's first three workshops in the TMS process. All teams and facilitators will adapt these agendas to fit their specific team needs, which will ensure they create Right-Minded Teamwork and achieve the TMS goals.

At the beginning of the TMS program's Phase 4, this sub-team will develop a fourth team-building agenda that teams will adapt and use for every 90-day team-building workshop after that.

See below: *5 Workshop Agendas for your RMT Implementation Plan* for agendas you may adopt or adapt for your TMS program. To purchase downloadable copies of these agendas, go to RightMindedTeamwork.com and search for this book's companion ***Reusable Resources & Templates***.

Reason, Ego, & the Right-Minded Teamwork Myth

The Philosophy & Process for
Creating a Right-Minded Team That Works as One

In this book, we explore two significant concepts:

- The RMT Myth, a short tale that presents RMT's underlying teamwork **philosophy**
- The RMT team-building **process**

The RMT Myth is a short, simple story.

It follows three characters: **Reason, Ego**, and you, the **Decision-Maker**. The myth illustrates the Right-Minded Teamwork philosophy, sort of like an aspirational thought system.

EGO   DECISION   REASON
             MAKER

Right-Minded Teammates Follow Reason

Simply put, the RMT Myth advocates for teammates to follow Reason's path to oneness and shared interest instead of following Ego's disastrous advice to seek separateness and prioritize selfishness.

In other words, the Right-Minded Teamwork Myth illustrates what "right-minded" thinking and behaving ideally look and feel like.

Once you have read and understood the RMT Myth, you and your team are ready for the Right-Minded Teamwork process.

Unlike the story about Reason, Ego, and the Decision-Maker, the RMT process is no myth. It is practical, deliberate, and reliable.

The RMT process is a set of interconnected, team-building methods that together form a self-perpetuating, continuous improvement system. It allows *you to integrate the aspirations of the RMT Myth into your team in a way that helps you achieve your business goals.*

This book will teach you the RMT process, including seven of RMT's proven team-building methods that lead to continuous improvement.

Pick up your free copy of the ebook at RightMindedTeamwork.com or your favorite book retailer. It is also available in paperback.

What Is "Right" in Right-Minded Teamwork?

It is worth stating and restating: Right-Minded Teamwork has nothing to do with right-brain thinking or right-wing viewpoints.

*RMT has everything to do with **what you and your teammates collectively decide is "right."***

Your team's choices on what acceptable work behavior and efficient processes look like define your team's Right-Minded Teamwork "thought system." The "right" way of doing, being, and behaving is the way that is right *for your team.*

The "right" way is how *your* team, and *your* organization, decide how all of you will **do no harm** and **work as one**.

So, how do you start the team's discussion about what is right or wrong?

Since your organization is deploying an *RMT Team Management System,* you will "start" each team's discussion as they enroll in the TMS program. During the team's one-hour TMS orientation, the team leader, teammates, and the team-building facilitator will meet and discuss the program and begin the team-building process.

5 Elements:
Right-Minded Teamwork in Any Team

Right-Minded Teamwork is a business-oriented, psychological approach to team building where acceptance, forgiveness, and adjustment are teammate characteristics, and 100% customer satisfaction is the team's result.

Your *RMT Team Management System* will apply Right-Minded Teamwork's 5 Elements in every team.

The model includes five interlocking elements, including two goals and three methods. During your team's first three workshops, you will integrate these 5 Elements into your operating system, ensuring you are doing your part to achieve your organization's goals and strategic plan.

The RMT 5 Elements are presented below, but to thoroughly learn the model and how to apply it, go to your favorite book retailer or RightMindedTeamwork.com, and pick up your copy of ***Right-Minded Teamwork in Any Team:*** *The Ultimate Team Building Method to Create a Team That Works as One.*

The 5 Elements: An Overview

1. Team **Business Goals** include your vision, mission, objectives, and customer satisfaction goals and plan.

2. Team **Psychological Goals** are your team's chosen "thought system." They incorporate your team's values, attitudes, and behaviors.

3. Team **Work Agreements** are your team's promises to follow agreed-upon work processes and interpersonal behaviors to help you achieve your business and psychological goals.

4. Your **Team Operating System** is the 90-day, continuous improvement system that ensures you stay focused and on track toward achieving your goals.

5. The **Right-Minded Teammate** is about developing and strengthening teammate skills and abilities to achieve both individual and team goals.

Let's take a closer look at the RMT 5 Elements and concepts now.

Element #1
Business Goal: Achieve 100% Customer Satisfaction

Clear goals focus your team.

For your team to succeed, each team member must first know, understand, and choose to align with the team's overarching performance goals, including the team's vision, mission, and charter.

Said another way, your team is responsible for providing products or services to customers. For the team and the enterprise to succeed, those customers must be satisfied, ideally 100% of the time. It is up to you and your team to identify the processes and behaviors that will get you there - the "right" way for your team. Additionally, teammates must see how their efforts contribute to the team's goals in order to be motivated to help achieve them.

Since 100% customer satisfaction is a nearly universal goal for teams, RMT focuses on guiding teams to achieve this goal.

Within the 5 Elements framework that forms Right-Minded Teamwork, the team's Business Goal is the first Element. This segment of RMT advocates these two tasks:

1. Ask your customer what 100% satisfaction means to them and create a plan to achieve it.
2. Make sure all team business goals align with your organization's strategic plan.

Without clear, aligned goals, team members may falter, become distracted, or fail to fulfill their role on the team. Identifying your Business Goal gets your team on the same page.

Element #2
Psychological Goal: Commit to Your Team's Right-Minded Thinking

Right-Minded Teamwork advocates a psychological approach to team building. Here's why:

Your attitudes and thoughts precede and cause your work behavior.

Therefore, when you choose Right-Minded thoughts and attitudes, your work behavior also shifts, naturally improving teamwork.

Commit to Your Team's Right-Minded Thinking

Psychological goals help your team align with your organization's stated values.

To achieve Right-Minded Teamwork, your team must first identify their "right" attitudes. These chosen attitudes form your team's collective, consciously chosen thought system.

Your team's initial set of Right-Minded Teamwork attitudes are created and agreed upon during the first RMT team-building workshop. After that, they may be adjusted and updated on an as-needed basis.

Your list of "right" attitudes can be short. Here is an example.

We choose these Right-Minded attitudes as our psychological goals:

- *We accept 100% accountability and responsibility for our thoughts and behaviors.*

- *When we make mistakes, we never punish. We do no harm. We work as one. We learn. We recover.*

- *We positively acknowledge and reward each other.*

- *We are we-centered, never self-centered.*

- *When difficult team situations happen, we accept, forgive, and adjust our attitudes and behavior. We always find solutions because we believe that none of us is as smart as all of us.*

- *When new teammates join our team, we will share these goals and ask them to choose them too.*

In that first RMT workshop, teammates work together to choose several psychological goals. Both the agreed-upon attitudes and the team's commitment to living them are captured in team Work Agreements.

Choosing Right Attitudes

To identify "right" attitudes and psychological goals for your team, you have two options:

1. Share the Right-Minded Teammate Attitudes & Behaviors list with the team and allow teammates to choose a few from that list. Or use those ideas to create goals that fit your team better.

   The list is below: *30 Right-Minded Teamwork Attitudes & Behaviors*.

2. Share the Right-Minded Teamwork Choice Model (as described in the *How to Apply the Right Choice Model* book). In a team workshop, agree on a list of accountable attitudes, and work behaviors your team believes are needed to successfully address your teamwork issues and to sustain RMT.

After you create these values and norms for your team, you must commit to living them, usually by capturing them in Work Agreements, the next Element of Right-Minded Teamwork.

 To Learn More...

See the **What Is the Right Choice Model?** section of this book.

Element #3
Work Agreements: Create & Follow
Your Commitments

A Work Agreement is a documented, team-building best practice. Work Agreements are one of the most reliable ways to create and sustain a unified team.

A Work Agreement is a covenant, promise, and pledge that transforms dysfunctional behavior into effective work behavior. It is not a flimsy ground rule. It is an emotionally mature promise that, when followed, will create and sustain cohesive teamwork. Simply put, Work Agreements turn adversaries into teammate allies.

Creating and following Work Agreements will:

1. Increase the likelihood your team will achieve 100% customer satisfaction
2. Define how the team will align with the organization's business strategy and stated values while pursuing 100% team customer satisfaction

When followed, Work Agreements ensure your team achieves its psychological and business goals. Work Agreements may also be used to resolve uncertainty, confusion, or conflict around roles, responsibilities, and work processes.

To create Work Agreements, leaders and teammates in team-building workshops openly discuss and agree on work performance behaviors that will clear up unresolved interpersonal or work process issues. These challenges are either already hurting the team, or they have the potential to hurt team performance.

Once the team's Right-Minded attitudes are defined, they are documented in team Work Agreements. When teammates align their choices and live their Agreements, their collaboration strengthens their ability to achieve customer satisfaction.

They work together as one.

Two Types of Work Agreements

Work Agreements resolve teamwork issues.

There are two types of Agreements.

A **process Work Agreement** describes who does what task and which work method they will use to perform that task.

A **behavioral Work Agreement** describes how people will behave while they carry out their tasks.

See the section *10 Steps: How to Facilitate Team Work Agreements* for an introduction to the 10 Steps facilitation process.

For complete guidance on establishing effective Work Agreements in your team, see the RMT book ***How to Facilitate Team Work Agreements***: *A Practical, 10-Step Process for Building a Right-Minded Team That Works as One.*

Element #4
Team Operating System:
Make Yours Effective & Efficient

A Right-Minded Teamwork Team Operating System is a 90-day, continuous improvement plan that ensures your team stays focused on achieving 100% customer satisfaction.

Your Team Operating System organizes your team processes and procedures. There are six components.

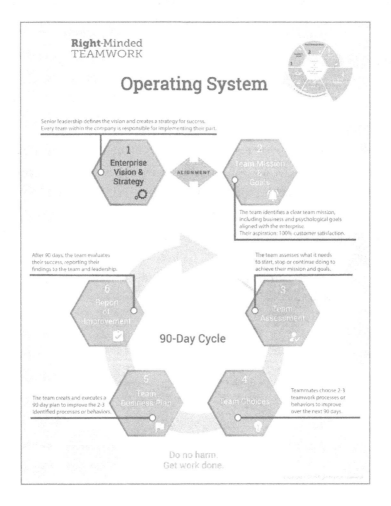

Six Steps: RMT's 90-Day Team Operating System

1. Enterprise Vision & Strategy
The senior leadership team creates the high-level vision and strategy. Every team within the organization is accountable for implementing their part.

2. Team Mission & Goals
Once teammates understand their team's responsibility and accountability to the enterprise's vision and strategy, they create a team mission, business goals, and psychological goals.

The team's mission and goals ensure the team focuses its energy and resources on achieving 100% customer satisfaction.

3. Team Assessment
With clear direction, the team conducts the *Team Performance Factor Assessment* to determine what the team needs to start, stop, or continue doing to achieve its mission and goals.

The team assessment identifies improvement opportunities. This review ensures the team stays focused and on track. This team assessment is re-administered every 90 days, and adjustments are made accordingly.

4. Team Choices
In this segment, teams determine their two to three critical-few projects, deliverables, or initiatives to achieve over the next 90 days.

These actions will improve these Team Performance Factors:
- Financial Goals
- Product or Service Quality
- Work Efficiency
- Teammate Relationships

They also choose how they will make progress toward those projects or goals, using one or more of RMT's three strategies:
1. Create process Work Agreements
2. Create behavioral Work Agreements
3. Implement an improvement project

You will find a more detailed description of each of these three strategies in the next section, *Three Team Improvement Strategies.*

5. Team Business Plan
All team choices, especially the two to three critical-few projects, are captured in a Team Business Plan, a document used to guide and track the team's efforts over the next 90 days (and every quarter after that).

6. Report of Improvement
Every 90 days, the team conducts another *Team Performance Factor Assessment,* and they calculate their actual performance improvement.

Based on assessment results, a Report of Improvement is created and presented to the team's sponsor or supervisor. In the improvement report, the team also captures key lessons learned as well as their best and worst practices. See the *5 Workshop Agendas* section for a Report of Improvement template.

Within your RMT Team Management System (TMS), all quarterly Reports of Improvement and lessons learned are shared with the TMS Steering Team.

Next, the team leader reinforces clarity by confirming the team's mission and goals align with company-driven objectives. If the team's objectives align with the company's objectives, the team repeats the continuous improvement system by examining *Team Performance Factor Assessment* results, identifying opportunities, and taking action on their findings.

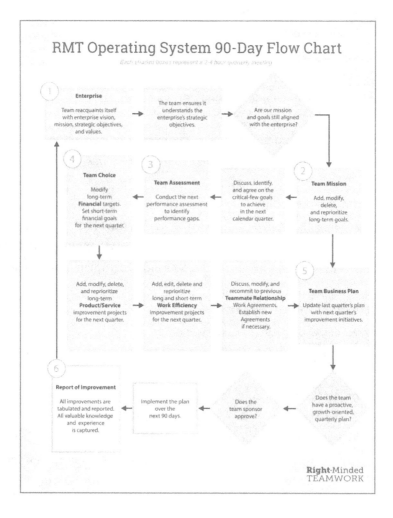

RMT Operating System 90-Day Flow Chart

Each shaded board represent a 2-4 hour quarterly meeting

1 Enterprise
Team reacquaints itself with enterprise vision, mission, strategic objectives, and values. → The team ensures it understands the enterprise's strategic objectives. → Are our mission and goals still aligned with the enterprise?

4 Team Choice
Modify long-term **Financial** targets. Set short-term financial goals for the next quarter. ← **3 Team Assessment** Conduct the next performance assessment to identify performance gaps. ← Discuss, identify, and agree on the critical-few goals to achieve in the next calendar quarter. ← **Team Mission 2** Add, modify, delete, and reprioritize long-term goals.

Add, modify, delete, and reprioritize long-term **Product/Service** improvement projects for the next quarter. → Add, edit, delete and reprioritize long and short-term **Work Efficiency** improvement projects for the next quarter. → Discuss, modify, and recommit to previous **Teammate Relationship** Work Agreements. Establish new Agreements if necessary. → **Team Business Plan 5** Update last quarter's plan with next quarter's improvement initiatives.

6 Report of Improvement
All improvements are tabulated and reported. All valuable knowledge and experience is captured. ← Implement the plan over the next 90 days. ← Does the team sponsor approve? ← Does the team have a proactive, growth-oriented, quarterly plan?

Right-Minded TEAMWORK

Three Team Improvement Strategies

As a team, teammates choose one or more of these strategies to help them make progress towards achieving projects or goals.

1. **Create Process Work Agreements**.
These Agreements usually improve ineffective processes and procedures. They may also clarify important teamwork topics, like roles and responsibilities or team meeting effectiveness.

The Agreements are discussed and agreed upon in a team workshop. Teammates follow these Agreements and, as a result, see an immediate positive impact.

Outcome: Process Work Agreements reduce workload, eliminate duplication, and add value to team products and services.

 To Learn More...

Go to the Resources section, and find *RMT Implementation Plan – 4 Actual Examples*. Read in Example #3 – International Project Team how this team's...

> **Process** *Work Agreement saved them USD $10,000 per week in labor costs.*

2. Create Behavioral Work Agreements.

These Agreements improve team relationships in essential areas such as increasing trust and respect or resolving workplace conflicts.

These Agreements are also created in a team workshop. Often, team members feel optimistic that their collective Agreements will benefit everyone. Teammates immediately follow these Agreements, though it usually takes a few weeks to a month of practice before the team begins to see positive results and improved team relationships.

Outcome: Behavioral Work Agreements improve teammate trust, increase risk-taking, and create team loyalty and accountability.

 To Learn More…

Go to the Resources section, and find *RMT Implementation Plan – 4 Actual Examples*. Read in Example #2 – Field Support Team how this team's…

> ***Behavioral*** *Work Agreement increased their trust for one another by 78%.*

3. **Implement an Improvement Project.**

An improvement project is also discussed and agreed upon in a team meeting, but it is more complicated than a Work Agreement.

A team Improvement Project will:
- Take a group of two or more teammates to resolve
- Need a thorough analysis before making a final decision
- Require two to 12 weeks to address and analyze thoroughly
- Use objective data like number of errors, cost per error, and categorization of mistakes (sorted by type and how urgently the error needs fixing)

Improvement Project examples:
1. Improve work scheduling efficiency
2. Improve customer and supplier communication
3. Reduce product and service mistakes
4. Improve the decision-making process and quality
5. Improve weak or inefficient pass-offs between customer and supplier teams
6. Fix the problem of missed customer deliveries due to inadequate communications between internal departments

 To Learn More...

Go to the Resources section, and find *RMT Implementation Plan – 4 Actual Examples*. Read in Example #1 – Nuclear Power Generating Plant how the senior leadership team's…

***Improvement Project**, a site-wide plan they named a 100-day Behavioral Outage, positively changed the organization's culture.*

Team Decision-Making

Before we discuss how to create your own Team Operating System, let's take a moment to learn how Right-Minded teams make good decisions that allow them to do no harm, work as one, and achieve 100% customer satisfaction.

In order to keep things clear, RMT encourages every team to have and abide by a Decision-Making Work Agreement. Without one, the team will likely encounter many unnecessary interpersonal dysfunctions and work mistakes. I'm confident your own experience has already shown you this is true, which is why it makes good business sense to create one and include it in your team's Operating System.

Decision-Making Work Agreements

A team's Decision-Making Work Agreement clearly defines how decisions are made and who makes them. RMT advocates every team create such a Decision-Making Work Agreement as early as possible, so if your team does not already have a Decision-Making Work Agreement, decision-making is an excellent topic to choose as the teamwork topic to address in your first RMT workshop. If you have a Decision-Making Agreement but have not updated it lately, make it a priority.

Once you have one, it's also a good idea in team meetings to remind teammates of your Decision-Making Work Agreement. Doing so will prevent many conflicts. Below you will find a description of several different decision-making approaches. Use these options to help you create an effective Agreement for your team. Incidentally, Decision-Making is #18 in the *Team Performance Factor Assessment,* which plays a key role in your Team Operating System. We'll review it in just a moment.

Range of Decision-Making Options

There is no one right way to construct your Decision-Making Agreement, but here are some guidelines and definitions that will help.

1. Command

In this option, the leader decides and announces their decision to teammates. This option is suitable for emergency situations and inconsequential types of decisions. Ideally, when the leader announces their choice, teammates will happily abide by the leader's decision.

2. Consult

The leader gathers information and recommendations in small group meetings or with others outside the team. As with the command option, teammates happily abide by the decision when the leader announces their choice.

3. Consensus

In this option, the team desires to reach a consensus. Everyone has equal authority to persuade and advocate for what they believe to be the best decision.

Consensus does not mean that everyone agrees. What it means is that everyone will *actively support the decision* in word and deed even if they did not get everything they wanted. By actively supporting the decision, teammates are living their RMT motto of *"none of us is as smart as all of us."*

Before the team discusses an issue, create a fallback decision-making option if the team cannot reach a consensus. For example, you might agree that the majority of votes wins. Or you could default to a Subject Matter Expert or the team leader to make the final decision in the case of no consensus. There is no perfect fallback but having one before discussing the problem that needs a decision is highly recommended.

4. Delegation

In this option, the leader gives the team or a subgroup the authority to decide *if* they adhere to specific guidelines and boundaries.

When the group announces their choice, the leader and teammates will abide by the group's decision.

Decision-Making Guidelines

Use some or all of these guidelines in your team Decision-Making Work Agreement.

An effective Decision-Making Work Agreement requires facilitating the team through two different activities. First, *define the problem* and, second, *solve the problem.*

For important decisions, always allow enough time to discuss the issue thoroughly to ensure you properly define the problem.

Frequently remind teammates of your RMT motto: *None of us is as smart as all of us.*

It's best to avoid debates. If you decide to play a devil's advocate role, announce it in advance.

It's also best not to immediately settle for majority rule, compromises, or trade-offs. Always go into every discussion by looking for a win-win solution.

It's best not to interpret a teammate's silence as support. For some decisions, ask each person to state out loud why they support the decision.

Decide what the group will tell others outside the team about the decision. If necessary, script a standard communication that all agree to follow.

Once they make the decision, the team must reach a consensus.

What Is Consensus?

Consensus is not the same as 100% agreement. It does mean that all teammates agree to *actively support the team's decision*, in word and deed, even though it might not be their personal choice.

How do you know you have reached a consensus? Each teammate can say with confidence:

> *My personal views and ideas have been listened to and seriously considered.*
>
> *I have openly listened to and seriously considered the ideas and views of every other team member.*
>
> *Whether or not this decision would have been my choice, I will actively support it and work towards its implementation and success.*

An Actual Decision-Making Work Agreement

In this book, you will find two real-world Work Agreement examples.

The first one is a behavioral Communication Agreement, and the other is the **Decision-Making Work Agreement** below.

I worked with this team for a few years. They were phenomenally successful because teammates passionately created and actively lived their Agreements day in and day out.

Process Agreement – Decision-Making Protocol

Team Choice: Intention Statement

2. We will go for consensus for all key team decisions, but our fallback will be that Maria [team leader] will decide if we cannot reach a consensus.

Conditions for Acceptance / Clarification

A. Before entering a discussion, we'll agree on the decision-making method and fall back, plus when [date] a decision will be made.

B. Before delving into a solution, we will create an opportunity or problem statement.

C. At the beginning of our discussion, we will determine boundaries & givens (i.e., time sensitivity; cost, hassle, impact, 80% or 100% perfect decision, etc.).

D. We provide a business case (appropriate justification) for our decision, including cost/benefit.

E. During our conversations, we will advocate and inquire. We will not hold back. For instance, we will acknowledge assumptions and facts.

F. To create the best solutions, we will also think about alternative ways to test our solution (Devil's Advocate).

G. If we find ourselves at an impasse, we will call a "time out" to calm down or acquire more technical information.

H. When a decision is made, we will accurately represent and support the decision.

I. We do this agreement because we want to improve teamwork and trust in one another.

J. We will hold ourselves and others accountable for living the letter and the spirit of this agreement; we will fine-tune it as necessary

Creating Your Team Operating System

RMT's Team Operating System is, as its name states, a systematic process. It always works when you follow it.

Once your team completes the first two 90-day iterations, the process will gain speed and momentum, making it much faster than the first time. Eventually, you will become so adept at the steps included in your 90-day iterations they will become second nature.

In summary, the steps are:

- Using the *Team Performance Factor Assessment*, choose two to three improvement opportunities for the next 90 days.
- Create effective solutions.
- Implement those solutions for the next 90 days.
- Ensure those solutions are self-sustaining.
- Repeat the process every 90 days.

After studying the *Team Performance Factors Assessment* below, you might think it asks too much or that it is too hard. Please, put that thought aside for a little while.

Remember, *you do not have to fix all parts* of your Operating System at once. You must only choose the most critical improvement opportunities to improve *now*. When you look at the performance factors, you will see a carefully planned process that will strengthen your current operations.

Team Performance Factor Assessment

RMT's Team Operating System is a six-step, 90-day, continuous improvement process that organizes your team functions to increase the likelihood of achieving customer satisfaction.

The system includes the *Team Performance Factor Assessment*, which you will use to help teammates identify two to three improvement opportunities every 90 days.

The 25 performance factors in this assessment are perfectly aligned with and thus effectively measure the six steps of your operating system. They measure all aspects of Right-Minded Teamwork.

Team Performance Factor Assessment Instructions

1. Each teammate reviews the 25 Team Performance Factors.

    Give teammates a few days to complete their assessment. Teammates return their completed assessment to the team leader or facilitator.

2. Each teammate places a checkmark next to the two to three performance factors they believe the team should address in the upcoming 90 days.

3. All assessments are tallied and distributed to all team members before the next 90-day RMT team-building workshop.

    In this workshop, teammates will review their *Team Performance Factor Assessment* results and choose the two to three performance factors the team will improve during the upcoming 90 days.

    The team repeats this process every 90 days.

Team Performance Factor Assessment

Step 1 – Enterprise Vision & Strategy

1. The enterprise's vision, strategy, and strategic objectives are clear, understandable, and agreeable to our team.
2. The enterprise's values are clearly stated and embraced by our team. We believe our psychological goals and our work agreements align with them.
3. Our team sponsor's strategic objectives are clear, understood, and aligned with those of the enterprise.
4. Our team understands its responsibility for achieving our sponsor's objectives.
5. Senior leadership, our team sponsor, and our team members communicate openly to ensure our team is doing its part to fulfill the enterprise's strategic plan.

Step 2 – Team Mission & Goals

6. Our team has a team mission and business and psychological goals that align with our sponsor's objectives.
7. All our teammates actively support our team's mission and goals.

Step 3 – Team Assessment

8. Our team follows a holistic team assessment process to evaluate business processes and teamwork relationships and identify improvements needed to achieve our team's mission and goals.
9. The team has a clear set of 90-day goals as well as potential long-term objectives.
10. Our team is consistently following a short and long-term team development plan, like Right-Minded Teamwork.

Step 4 – Team Choices

11. Our **Financial Performance** – Our team has a budget or P&L.
12. Each team member understands their role in the team's financial performance.

13. Our **Product/Service Quality** – Each team member understands our team's deliverables and can adequately explain the features and benefits to anyone.
14. Our team has a process in place for continually improving our team's product and service offerings.

15. Our **Work Process Efficiencies** – Every teammate understands, accepts, and supports our team's operating systems and reporting responsibilities.
16. Our team has established effective and efficient work processes that will achieve our mission and business goals.
17. All teammates are clear about their roles, responsibilities, and accountability.
18. All teammates understand, accept, and support the team's decision-making process and protocols.
19. Our team meetings are practical and efficient. We update our Team Business Plan in team meetings, which tracks actual team performance and lessons learned.

20. Our **Team Relationships** – Each team member holds themselves and others accountable for following our team's psychological goals, our company values and team Work Agreements.
21. Each team member and the team's sponsor agree to do what they can to improve team unity, collaboration, and alignment.

Step 5 – Team Business Plan

22. Our team captures all Agreements, projects, action items, and improvement ideas in a Business Plan that is updated minimally every calendar quarter.

Step 6 – Report Improvement; Capture Knowledge

23. Every 90 days, our team conducts another team assessment that calculates and reports our actual performance improvement while also recognizing and acknowledging individual and group efforts. The assessment report is presented to our team's sponsor.
24. Additionally, the report includes our critical lessons learned and the best and worst practices from the previous quarter.

    If the enterprise has a central depository for lessons learned, the report is forwarded to that department.

25. Finally, our team leader ensures that our team's mission and goals align with our sponsor's objectives.

    Presuming they are, our team repeats the 90-day continuous improvement process, beginning with the *Team Performance Factor Assessment.*

Note: To see an abbreviated version of how a real team used Performance Factors, go to the Resources section at the end of this book, and find *Example #2: Field Support Team.*

To purchase a downloadable copy of the *Team Performance Factor Assessment* to distribute to your teammates, go to RightMindedTeamwork.com, and search for this book's **Reusable Resources & Templates** companion.

Element #5
Right-Minded Teammates:
Strengthen Individual Performance

Are you seeking satisfied customers? Do you want to work with collaborative and enjoyable teammates? Do you wish you were part of a team where trust and respect thrive, conflicts are mutually resolved, and teammates support each other in growing their skills and talents?

As a teammate, Right-Minded Teamwork gives you tools to improve your teamwork experience by delivering all these results and more.

Right-Minded Teamwork for Individuals

Working in a Right-Minded team strengthens your ability to be mindful, present, and available for the work at hand.

Rather than waking up each morning in a panic, dreading what the day may bring, you wake up feeling your work is important and valuable. Your contributions matter. Knowing this brings you happiness and joy. Your deep satisfaction helps you enthusiastically greet the day ahead.

When you go to sleep each evening, that feeling of fulfillment calms your mind. You are full of gratitude, honored to work with such incredible people. You are surrounded by teammates who, each day, demonstrate right-minded attitudes and behaviors. RMT allows your team to meet and possibly exceed individual and team goals consistently.

The 10 Characteristics of Right-Minded Teammates

Right-Minded Teammates have diverse backgrounds, vastly different experiences, and display a wide range of skills. No two are alike. Still, there are certain characteristics all Right-Minded Teammates share.

These characteristics align the teammate's authentic self with the RMT motto of *Do no harm, and work as one*. They are:

1. Trust
2. Honesty
3. Tolerance
4. Gentleness
5. Joy
6. Defenselessness
7. Generosity
8. Patience
9. Open-mindedness
10. Faithfulness

When you help your team create and live team Work Agreements, they will be well on their way to living these characteristics.

How does the Right-Minded Teammate live these characteristics?

They do two things when difficult situations occur.

First, they remind themselves of their commitment to *thinking* in a do-no-harm way. Second, they choose to demonstrate do-no-harm behaviors that align with their Right-Minded attitudes, such as finding solutions to challenging situations.

It is not always easy to do these two things, but it is always that simple.

To encourage your team to embrace and live these Right-Minded characteristics, check out these two RMT books:

7 Mindfulness Training Lessons*: Improve Teammates' Ability to Work as One with Right-Minded Thinking* will teach you how to apply RMT's seven, powerful thinking lessons to encourage Right-Minded, unified teamwork.

How to Apply the Right Choice Model*: Create a Right-Minded Team That Works as One* teaches you how to transform a disappointed team customer into a 100% satisfied customer by making Right-Minded choices, all of which align with the above list of characteristics.

For now, though, let's take a closer look at each of these 10, Right-Minded Teammate characteristics.

1. Trust

Trust is the foundational characteristic for teammates who desire to create and sustain Right-Minded Teamwork. Right-Minded Teammates trust one another because their own past experience has taught them that, in all situations, a forgiving attitude creates safety for teammates to collaborate and resolve difficulties.

2. Honesty

For the Right-Minded Teammate, honesty means more than just telling the truth. It refers to consistency in thought and deed. An honest, Right-Minded Teammate is consistently looking within and striving to align thoughts, words, and behaviors with the team's psychological goals and forgiving values. This kind of honesty is essential to creating and sustaining Right-Minded Teamwork.

3. Tolerance

Judgment is the opposite of forgiveness; it implies a lack of trust. Tolerance indicates non-judgment. Tolerant teammates do not judge one another because they know that though they are not the same, all Right-Minded Teammates are equal. Their tolerance creates space for the wisdom of diversity to surface, and their equality allows them to work together as one.

4. Gentleness

Right-Minded Teammates believe that gentleness is the only sane response to challenging situations and circumstances. Whereas harshness and judgment close doors, gentleness opens them. With gentleness, it is easy for teammates to do no harm as they work as one – with teammates and customers alike.

5. Joy

Joy is the inevitable result for Right-Minded teammates who are gentle and non-judgmental. Fear is impossible for those who are gentle, especially during challenging situations. Joy comes from gentleness, tolerance, honesty, and forgiveness.

6. Defenselessness

Right-Minded Teammates understand that defenses are foolish, judgmental attitudes and behaviors that prevent the team from finding solutions to difficult situations. When teammates summon the courage to forgive and trust themselves and to look honestly at their wrong-minded defenses without judgment, they can lay those debilitating arguments gently aside, creating the proper conditions for honestly doing no harm and working as one.

7. Generosity

Right-Minded Teammates honestly and humbly give all they know to help their team create Right-Minded Teamwork and achieve 100% customer satisfaction. The world teaches that if you give something away, you lose it, but Right-Minded Teammates realize that to give is to receive. They eagerly participate with their teammates to create solutions to solve challenging situations, bringing joy and satisfaction to the team through their gentle generosity.

8. Patience

Teammates who know Right-Minded Teamwork is the outcome they want can easily afford to wait without concern. Because their goal is to be tolerant and gentle with their teammates, patience comes naturally. The highest desire is to work as one.

9. Open-Mindedness

Judgment, or wrong-mindedness, closes teammates' minds, creating resistance for Right-Minded Teamwork. To ensure they do no harm while working as one, Right-Minded Teammates embrace open-mindedness, also known as Right-Mindedness.

10. Faithfulness

Faithfulness describes a teammate's trust in their team's version of Right-Minded Teamwork. When a teammate is faithful, they effortlessly and wholeheartedly believe in Right-Minded Teamwork. They *want* to do no harm and work as one. They know none of us is as smart as all of us. When applied during challenging circumstances, their faithfulness inevitably leads the team to happy outcomes.

Aspiring to Be a Right-Minded Teammate

Every teammate brings two talents to their team: **technical skill** and **personal attitude**.

RMT acknowledges that individuals possess a wide range of technical skills. For example, one teammate could possess strong computer skills while another has exceptional customer service skills. It is not practical to ask the customer service teammate to learn how to fix computers; RMT advocates putting teammates in jobs that best suit their technical skills.

Regardless of their specific roles, Right-Minded Teammates put effort into improving their skills. They also consciously embrace Right-Minded attitudes throughout their workday, focusing their attention on doing the right things the right way, with the right attitude.

When things go wrong, or they realize they are doing the right things the wrong way or with the wrong attitude, Right-Minded Teammates self-adjust their attitude and behavior, usually through a **moment of Reason.**

Combining Technical Skills & Right-Minded Attitudes

One of the best available tools for building teamwork is the book *Right-Minded Teamwork: 9 Right Choices for Building a Team That Works as One.*

Of the nine choices, the seventh choice is:

Mistakes happen. Correct them; don't punish people.

In this choice, when mistakes occur, teammates are asked to trust Reason above Ego. Too often, our instinctual reaction is to criticize, point fingers, or deny responsibility.

But if teams are to work as one, the mistake of one is also the mistake of the whole team.

Rather than blaming the person who made a mistake, Reason encourages you to rise above the battleground to a place in your mind that is strictly solution-focused, not blame-based. (To learn the full story about Reason, pick up our free ebook *Reason, Ego & the Right-Minded Teamwork Myth* at RightMindedTeamwork.com or your favorite book retailer. Also available in paperback.)

Despite your differences and their inadvertent error, Reason knows you and your teammate have the same goal. The only way forward is to accept what has happened, forgive all involved, and make the necessary adjustments to prevent it from happening again. Focusing on solutions that move you both towards that goal allows you to rise above your differences and work together. Ultimately, this shift helps strengthen individual and team performance.

For example, if a teammate skilled with computers spots a mistake made by a customer service teammate, instead of reacting with anger or blaming the customer service expert, the computer expert could extend an offer to help.

If treated with empathy and understanding, how would the customer service expert respond? Rather than feeling a need to shut down or become defensive, the customer service expert would likely be grateful, if a bit surprised, to receive the genuine offer of support. Together, they could find a way to correct the error and recover.

In this example, the Right-Minded attitude of correcting mistakes and the Right-Minded skill of proper communication brought the situation to an amicable, productive close.

Two Methods for Strengthening Individual Performance

In most cases, it is best to address individual teammate development *after* teammates have participated in the first two RMT team-building workshops (see Right-Minded Teamwork's three-workshop Implementation Plan below). By the time the team has two workshops under their belt, the team's goals and Work Agreements should already be well established. These team goals and Work Agreements inform how and why individual teammates desire to improve their performance, which plays directly into the fifth Element, Right-Minded Teammates.

Once you are ready to focus on improving individual performance within your team, you can:
- Conduct a Right-Minded Teammate development workshop
- Implement one-on-one coaching or training

Let's take a brief look at each option.

Conduct a Right-Minded Teammate Development Workshop

To improve team performance, have all teammates participate in a training workshop designed to improve a specific work skill or interpersonal talent.

Examples of work or technical skill development include:
- Boosting team meeting effectiveness through facilitation skills training
- Implementing process improvement training, like Six Sigma
- Using strategic planning exercises, like the Balanced Performance Scorecard
- Improving team problem-solving and decision-making through Kepner Tregoe training

Examples of interpersonal or attitude development include:
- Clarifying teammate roles and responsibilities using RMT's Role Clarification Exercise
- Improving teammate thinking and effectiveness by practicing RMT's 7 Mindfulness Training Lessons
- Learning about teammate characteristics through personality assessment tools - or try the much quicker exercise RMT's About Me & My Preferences Exercise
- Training teammates how to be assertive (not aggressive or passive) in their communications
- Increasing teammate trust by participating in a Speed of Trust training program or taking part in RMT's Trust Dialogue Exercise

These various RMT exercises can be found in several RMT books, including **Right-Minded Teamwork in Any Team**: *The Ultimate Team Building Method to Create a Team That Works as One.*

Implement Individual Coaching or Training

When brainstorming development ideas, it's natural for a Right-Minded Teammate to identify individual technical skills or talents they would like to improve.

Examples include:
- Learning a new software program or how to operate a new piece of equipment
- Studying for and obtaining a technical certification
- Attending a management or leadership training program
- Learning negotiation, mediation, or crisis management skills
- Improving the ability to communicate with difficult or angry people effectively

Since most work teams already conduct annual individual performance management assessments, RMT recommends each teammate record at least one personal development goal per year in their performance management program.

An individual development goal might be any of the above examples; however, RMT advocates all Right-Minded teammates include "developing Right-Minded Thinking" as one of their goals.

Onboarding New Teammates

When a new person, leader, or teammate, joins your team, it is vitally important to properly onboard them within their first week on the job. In a single short meeting where everyone attends, the onboarding is easily and effectively accomplished. Present all your RMT goals and Work Agreements along with why they were created. They ask you clarifying questions. Afterward, you ask them to accept the team's goals and actively live the team's Work Agreements.

Benefits of Right-Minded Teamwork

RMT is a real-world method that has profited thousands of people worldwide.

Ultimately, RMT is for everyone, everywhere, forever. It is universal, self-evident, and self-validating.

Praise for Right-Minded Teamwork

A fast read that takes you straight to the root of team dysfunctions and gives you proven, step-by-step tools to improve team function and deliver results. I have paid thousands of dollars for team trainings and workshops that are better summarized here. I am glad to be reminded to choose Reason over Ego and stay in my right mind.

Robin Hensley, VP IT, UPS

The author of this guide is all-knowing and has clearly and in a pithy way documented the nine steps to bringing a team together: that togetherness and one-mindedness are key elements to an average team doing extraordinary things. Your work provides a roadmap to use in building a team that works. Again, thank you. I always enjoyed our time together and appreciate all you did for me and my teams.

Alan Kleier, Former GM/VP, Chevron

In Right-Minded Teamwork, Dan separates the fun and games of team bonding from the hard work (the muck and mire) of team building. He presents an in-depth model for real-world team building in a realistic, direct, and safe manner. This is a book that you will use and wear out. Right-Minded Teamwork is also a support system, providing a rich array of resources.

Patrick Carmichael, VP Best Practices Institute, Former Head Talent Management, Saudi Aramco

What's great about the book is that in addition to the process outlined, the author provides supplemental resources and links to additional information to help you out.

Lauren Bailey, Project Leader, Boston Consulting Group

I successfully used the principles of Right-Minded Teamwork in a community mediation. I recommend Right-Minded Teamwork to any mediator engaged in dysfunctional behavior in community mediation.

Rick Murray, JD/Ph.D. Exec. Director, Dispute Resolution Center of the Northwest

Four Real Examples

For four, real-world success stories illustrating this multi-workshop plan, look for the *RMT Implementation Plan – 4 Actual Examples* in the Resources section.

5 Elements:
RMT Implementation Plan

Orientation + Three Workshops + 90-Day Operating System

Overview

There is no one right way to implement RMT. However, this plan has proven effective countless times.

Combining orientation, three team-building workshops, and a 90-day Team Operating System will ensure you succeed in creating a team that works together as one.

In the next section, we'll dive a bit deeper, but for now, here is a quick, high-level view of the five steps or phases of RMT's 5 Elements Implementation Plan:

1. **Team Orientation Meeting & Workshop Preparation**
   - Team leader & facilitator prepare for team orientation
   - Conduct a short orientation meeting and assign teammate preparation tasks

2. **First Workshop – Work Agreements**
   - Identify team psychological goals and values (Element #2)
   - Create at least one team Work Agreement (Element #3)
   - Identify one to two improvement projects for the next 90 days

3. **Second Workshop – Operating System**
   - Reset and reaffirm business goals (Element #1) and agree on the Team Operating System (Element #4)

4. **Third Workshop - Teammates**
   - Conduct a Right-Minded Teammate development workshop (Element #5)

5. **90-Day Operating Plan – Ongoing**
   - Every 90 days, conduct another *Team Performance Factor Assessment*. The team meets to assess progress, identify opportunities, take action, and achieve new teamwork improvements.

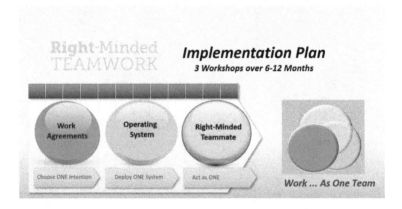

Workshop Preparation & Team Orientation Meeting

Whether you are implementing RMT in your team for its own sake or as part of your TMS rollout, the process begins when the team leader and the team-building facilitator prepare for their team's orientation meeting and then conduct the session.

Given the prevalence of virtual teams, the first decision to make is whether to conduct an in-person event or a virtual workshop. In virtual workshops, the same principles, concepts, and steps apply, but an **in-person workshop is highly recommended**. Being physically in the same room gives teammates a chance to see and feel other teammates' attitudes and behaviors.

If a virtual format is necessary, use a video software conferencing platform to ensure all participants can see each other as well as the virtual flip chart you will use to capture your team Work Agreements.

As one of your first steps, it is essential to assess your team's current performance. This could be a subjective or an objective assessment. An excellent option is the RMT *Team Performance Factor Assessment* discussed in *Element #4 – Team Operating System*.

When rolling out RMT as part of your TMS, before the orientation meeting, give teammates this memo: ***An Orientation: Introducing our Team Management System (TMS).*** This memo explains the TMS program. In the next section, you will find a template, which you may adopt or adapt to fit your needs.

In the orientation meeting, teammates learn about and discuss RMT's 5 Elements, the three-workshop implementation approach, the 90-day operating process, and the creation of team Work Agreements that will help them improve their teamwork.

Teammates learn the facilitator will guide the team in the first three workshops and co-facilitate their fourth. At that time, the facilitator will turn over the facilitation duties to the team going forward.

The leader and facilitator then raise the topic of choosing the team's one to two teamwork topics to address in their first workshop. Teammates learn the facilitator will interview them before the first workshop, and collectively, they will finalize the first topics to address. They also agree on the first workshop date.

For many teams, the first workshop typically focuses on team cohesion and unity. Often a lack of cohesion or unity is the underlying cause of poor performance that created your team's improvement opportunities.

Workshop 1 – Psychological Goals & Work Agreements

In the first team workshop, under the leader and facilitator's guidance, your team works together to clarify and agree on its psychological goals or team values and create one or more Work Agreements to address the chosen teamwork topics.

Work Agreements, created collectively by and agreed upon by all team members, ensure everyone operates under a single set of performance and behavioral expectations. Work Agreements are powerfully effective at resolving interpersonal issues and work process conflicts.

When your team creates and follows its first set of Agreements, it is an "early win" for the team because teammates resolve essential issues while also setting a positive, we-can-do-this tone for future successes.

Here's a real-life "early win" story. A major capital project team immediately saved $10,000 a week in labor costs when they successfully used RMT's **process Work Agreement** to streamline their meetings. For details, at the end of this book, look for *Example #3 – International Project Team in the RMT Implementation Plan – 4 Actual Examples* section. All four examples show you clear evidence that Work Agreements work.

To help you on your way to achieving an "early win," you can use the list of *30 Right-Minded Teamwork Attitudes & Behaviors*, discussed later, to assist in choosing your team's psychological goals and desired work behaviors.

Additionally, teammates may be asked to read ***Right-Minded Teamwork****: 9 Right Choices for Building a Team That Works as One.*
Doing so is optional, but this short and easy-to-read book will help foster an attitude of "Right-Mindedness" among all teammates.

Teams often experience a boost in productivity and motivation from the first workshop alone because they immediately see the positive benefits of the Right-Minded Teamwork model.

Workshop 2 – Business Goals & Operating System

Once psychological goals and initial Work Agreements are in place, you are ready for the second workshop. This event, which takes place two to four weeks after the first workshop, revolves around clarifying your business goals and establishing an effective Team Operating System.

Often, one of your business goals is to achieve 100% customer satisfaction. Your team must agree on what this kind of success looks like for your customer. Additionally, it is crucial that you validate your conclusions with your team's customers.

Validating your assumptions means ensuring all teammates know and understand not only the expectations of your team's direct customers but also the expectations of *their customers.*

> *When your team helps your customers achieve 100% satisfaction with their customers, you will most certainly have achieved a prosperous and successful working relationship.*

You will find instructions for creating a customer satisfaction plan in the RMT book, ***Right-Minded Teamwork in Any Team****: The Ultimate Team-Building Method to Create a Team That Works as One.*

With a clear business goal and united focus, you are ready to discuss and create an actionable plan to strengthen work performance and eliminate wasted time and effort.

In this second team-building workshop, you will identify one to three opportunities to improve your Team Operating System over the next 90 days.

Just as Work Agreements guide team behavior, the Team Operating System defines (or redefines) your team's structure. Your continuous improvement operating system uses the *Team Performance Factor Assessment* to help your team identify improvement opportunities such as roles, responsibilities, and team processes and procedures.

This second workshop continues to build momentum by delivering more evidence that the RMT model is working.

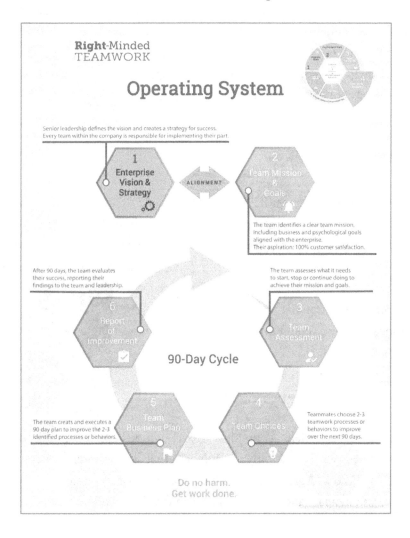

Workshop 3 – Teammate Growth & Development

Now that teammates have experienced more productive teamwork from the first two workshops, you are ready to conduct the third workshop focused on individual growth and development.

In this workshop, which takes place two to four months after the second workshop, teammates are encouraged to take an honest look at their attitudes, behaviors, and work performance. They are asked to identify simple, legitimate, and actional improvements that will not only improve individual performance but will help improve the team's collective performance. Improvement goals are then shared with teammates to not only validate them but to encourage wholehearted support.

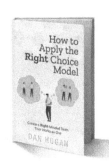

For this workshop, you have a variety of training options. You might choose to instruct teammates more thoroughly in RMT's *Right Choice Model* or the *7 Mindfulness Training Lessons*. You could invite a professional to teach a new work process that would enhance the team's work efficiencies. You could also request a behavioral training specialist to teach such things as how to communicate during conflicts.

The outcome of this workshop is to identify actionable improvements for each person.

After you complete your third RMT workshop, you and your teammates will be totally convinced that your Team Operating System, Work Agreements, and customer satisfaction mission will ensure you create and sustain Right-Minded Teamwork.

Approximately 90 days after your third workshop (and every 90 days after that), your team will follow your Team Operating Plan (created in the second workshop) to assess team progress, identify new improvement opportunities, take action, and achieve greater team success.

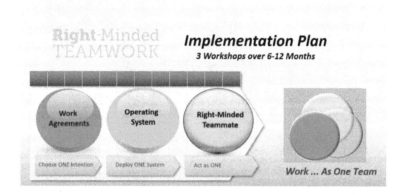

 To Learn More...

For four real-world success stories illustrating this multi-workshop plan, go to the Resources section at the end of this book, and find *RMT Implementation Plan – 4 Actual Examples.*

Want better teamwork?

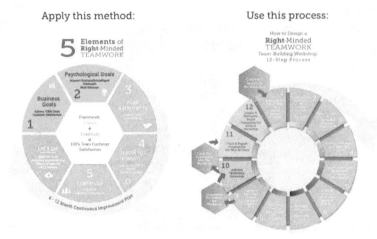

Benefits of RMT's Orientation + Three-Workshop + 90-Day Implementation Plan

When you implement RMT as suggested, whether through the three consecutive team-building workshops plus the 90-day operating system or in a manner of your choosing, your TMS teams will be well on their way to sustaining an efficient operating plan for high-performance teamwork and improved teammate relationships.

Most importantly, your teams and your organization will consistently accomplish business goals and achieve customer satisfaction. Everyone will be doing their part to help the enterprise achieve its strategic plan.

5 Workshop Agendas for
Your RMT Implementation Plan

In this section, you will find a sample teammate orientation memo and some valuable agendas that you may use and reuse in your TMS program.

Go to RightMindedTeamwork.com to download these materials.

Memo Template
An Orientation:
Introducing Our Team Management System

What is our Team Management System (TMS)?

Our new Team Management System aims to align all teammate goals, attitudes, and work behaviors to ensure everyone is on the same page and doing their part to achieve our vision, mission, and strategic goals.

How does TMS work?

TMS is much like our employee performance management system, just on a team level.

The TMS is a top-to-bottom process, which means every team will participate from the executive leadership team and throughout the organization. Instead of individual evaluations, every team will set performance goals that are aligned with our strategic plan. Teams will measure and report their actual results every quarter, and they will set new goals for the upcoming quarter.

We have created a TMS Steering Team that will manage the program for the first two years. After that, we will create a permanent department that will lead and manage our TMS.

There are four sub-teams who are ready and able to support you right now:

- The *TMS Liaison Team* is the primary point of contact between the Executive Team, the Steering Team, and the entire organization.

- The *RMT Facilitator Training Team* identifies and trains our very own facilitators.

- The *RMT Facilitator Assignment Team* is the clearinghouse for receiving team-building support requests.

- The *RMT Implementation Design Team* builds and refines our organization's standard, team-building process.

What are the benefits?

With TMS, every team in our organization operates with clarity and focus, allowing us to consistently achieve a higher percentage of our strategic goals year over year.

How long does it take to reap the benefits?

Within the first six to 12 months, our TMS will not only begin paying for itself, but we will also see evidence of organizational performance improvement. Within the first 18 to 24 months, the TMS will report consistent and demonstrable enterprise-wide results.

Who participates?

- Executive Leadership Team
- TMS Steering Team
- Internal (possibly external) team-building facilitators
- All teams will eventually participate

Right-Minded Teamwork – Our Standard Teamwork Process

Right-Minded Teamwork is a real-world and practical approach.

A real-world approach to team building is better for our TMS because it addresses and resolves real team issues. It is also the most reliable way to achieve and sustain high-performance teamwork.

Our TMS will apply **Right-Minded Teamwork's 5 Elements.**

RMT's 5 Elements model includes five interlocking elements, including two goals and three methods. Over the first six to nine months of our TMS, your team will integrate these 5 Elements in your team's operating systems, ensuring you are doing your part to achieve our organization's goals and strategic plan. You will learn more about Right-Minded Teamwork and the 5 Elements model in the TMS orientation meeting.

5 Elements of **Right**-Minded TEAMWORK

Psychological Goals
Achieve Emotionally-Intelligent Teammate Work Behavior

2

3
Work Agreements
Create and Follow Commitments

Business Goals
Achieve 100% Team Customer Satisfaction

1

Framework:
2 Goals
+
3 Methods
=
100% Team Customer Satisfaction

4
Operating System
Build an Effective & Efficient Operating System

Let's go!
Apply the Three Workshop Implementation Plan to incorporate all 5 Elements

5
Teammate
Strengthen Individual Performance

6 - 12 Month Continuous Improvement Plan

The Right-Minded Teamwork Philosophy

The Right-Minded Teamwork philosophy is founded on two universal truths:

None of us is as smart as all of us.
Right-Minded Teammates know that working collaboratively together, in a Right-Minded manner, is the only way to create the kind of teamwork that achieves and sustains 100% customer satisfaction.

Do no harm and work as one.
As a Right-Minded Teammate, you can be firm, direct, gentle, and compassionate, all at the same time. You do not blame yourself or others for mistakes; you find and implement solutions. You and your teammates are allies, not adversaries. You work together towards your shared goals.

Do you want everyone in our organization to work as one?

Our Executive Team and extended leadership team have already given this question a resounding "yes!"

We also believe that every person in our organization has a special function: to strengthen your individual and collective team's Right-Minded Thinking and to show everyone else, by your example, how to do the same.

How do you strengthen your Right-Minded Thinking? Among other things, you actively live and demonstrate the Right-Minded Teamwork attitudes and behaviors that will be presented to you later in the TMS process. You and your teammates will choose to adapt or adopt those attitudes and behaviors as you see fit.

Changing Our Future by Changing Our Minds

Our TMS program is asking everyone to choose to do two things:
1. Do no harm
2. Work as one

When we all act and behave this way, we do our part to make our organization and the world a little bit better for everyone, everywhere.

That said, we are pragmatic. We accept we cannot single handedly change or transform most of the civil unrest in the world. But we can and should transform our attitudes and behaviors by committing to "do no harm" and "work as one."

The more we train our minds to accept this philosophy, the more we realize that choosing anything but working together as one unified team and organization is nothing but foolishness.

You already know, from your own experience, that "doing no harm and working as one" is the way forward. Within your team and yourself, these words must be said, then repeated many times. At first, they will be partially accepted with many reservations, but over time, they will be considered seriously, more and more, until finally "Do no harm. Work as one," is accepted as truth.

When our organization achieves and sustains our version of Right-Minded Teamwork, we will be doing our part to transform our world into a better place for everyone, everywhere.

Sincerely,
TMS Steering Team

TMS Orientation Meeting – Enrolling a New Team

	TMS Orientation Meeting Date: Time: Location:
Attendees	List all teammates
Please Read	An Orientation: Introducing our **Team Management System**

Purpose & Desired Outcomes

Purpose: To enroll your team in our Team Management System

Desired Outcomes
1. Present, clarify, and understand our Team Management System and how it will help us achieve our Strategic Plan.
2. Introduce you to your team facilitator.
3. Present and understand how your team will apply our standard Right-Minded Teamwork process.
4. Discuss and agree on one or two teamwork topics to address in your first team-building workshop.
5. Schedule your first workshop and assign any essential teammate preparation tasks.

Agenda		
What	Who	When
Welcome & Kick-Off • Share purpose, the desired outcome • Review agenda	Team Leader	10-15 min
Team Management System - Overview • Present the TMS and answer questions • Introduce our team's facilitator • Learn that our team will conduct quarterly team-building workshops	Team Leader, Facilitator	
Right-Minded Teamwork • Briefly present our standard Right-Minded Teamwork process that includes 5 RMT Elements, the 5 Element Implementation Plan and the create of team Work Agreements		
Choose our first one or two topics • Brainstorm and list potential teamwork topics we believe if addressed will improve our team's performance • Discuss and agree on one or two topics to address in our first workshop	Facilitator	
Closure • Schedule our first workshop and assign any needed teammate preparation tasks • Share any acknowledgments or appreciations	Team Leader, Facilitator	

First Workshop – Psychological Goals & Work Agreements

	TMS: 1ˢᵗ Team-Building Workshop Date: Time: Location:
Attendees	List all teammates
Please Read	***Right-Minded Teamwork:** 9 Right Choices for Building a Team That Works as One,* especially this section: *30 Right-Minded Teamwork Attitudes & Behaviors*
Please Bring	Your ideas on how to successfully address our agreed-upon team topics

Purpose & Desired Outcomes

Purpose: Create and sustain our version of Right-Minded Teamwork

Desired Outcomes
1. Discuss and agree on our psychological team goals and values (RMT Element #2)

2. Discuss and create Work Agreements (RMT Element #3) as to how we will improve [first team topic]

3. Discuss and agree on how to improve [second team topic]

Agenda		
What	Who	When
Welcome & Kick-Off • Share purpose, the desired outcome • Review agenda, meeting behavior, agreements	Team Leader, Facilitator	10-15 min
Our Teams Psychological Goals & Values • Present and briefly discuss Right Choice Model • Discuss and agree on our psychological goals/values by adapting some of RMT's 30 Right-Minded Teamwork Attitudes & Behaviors		
First Team Topic • Define the problem • Solve the problem; create Work Agreement		
Second Team Topic • Define the problem • Solve the problem; create Work Agreement		
Closure • List workshop positives as well as things to do differently in the next workshop • Schedule the second workshop within 2-4 weeks; brainstorm topics to address • Review/commit to Agreements & Actions • Acknowledgments & appreciations		

Second Workshop – Business Goals & Operating System

	TMS: 2nd Team-Building Workshop Date: Time: Location:
Attendees	List all teammates
Please Read	***Right-Minded Teamwork in Any Team:*** *The Ultimate Team Building Method to Create a Team That Works as One,* especially this section: *Element #4 Team Operating System: Make Yours Efficient.* Choose two to four topics from RMT's ***Team Performance Factor Assessment*** that you believe will improve your team's Operating System
Please Bring	Your ideas on how to successfully address our agreed-upon team topics and improve our Team Operating System

Purpose & Desired Outcomes

Purpose: Create and sustain our version of Right-Minded Teamwork

Desired Outcomes
1. Discuss, clarify, understand and agree on our team business goals (RMT Element #1)

2. Discuss and agree on how to improve our team Operating System (RMT Element #4)

Agenda		
What	Who	When
Welcome & Kick-Off • Share purpose, the desired outcome • Review agenda, meeting behavior, agreements	Team Leader, Facilitator	10-15 min
Our Teams Business Goals • Present all of the team's current business goals – team leader • All teammates discuss, clarify, modify if needed and agree on all of our business goals • We also commit to achieving 100% customer satisfaction and we will create a plan our customer(s) support	Team Leader, Facilitator	
Our Team Operating System • List all teammate choices from RMT's *Team Performance Factor Assessment* • Discuss & agree on the top two to three "factors" to improve over the next 90-days. • Create any needed Work Agreements or improvement projects that will improve our team Operating System		
Closure • List workshop positives as well as things to do differently in the next workshop • Schedule the third workshop and brainstorm a list of 1-3 teammate development topics • Review/commit to Agreements & Action Plan • Acknowledgments & appreciations		

Third Workshop – Teammate Growth & Development

	TMS: 3ʳᵈ Team-Building Workshop Date: Time: Location:
Attendees	List all teammates
Please Read	***About Me & My Preferences*** Team-Building Exercise and Instructions [see below]
Please Bring	…your answer to one of the preference questions

Purpose & Desired Outcomes

Purpose: Create and sustain our version of Right-Minded Teamwork

Desired Outcome

1. Present, clarify, understand and agree as to how we will "work as one" with each teammate's personal work preferences (RMT Element #5)

Agenda		
What	Who	When
Welcome & Kick-Off • Share purpose, the desired outcome • Review agenda, meeting behavior, agreements	Team Leader, Facilitator	10-15 min
Teammate – My Preferences • A teammate will share their answer to one preference question: 1-2 minutes • Teammates ask clarifying questions: 5-10 min • If all agree they can actively support that preference, close the discussion. Move on. • If some find it challenging to support that work preference, the team will discuss and find an acceptable way for all teammates to "work as one" to accommodate everyone's work preference. • Create a written Work Agreements to be certain it's clear and will be remembered • Close discussion and move to the next teammate and repeat the process above		
Closure • List workshop positives as well as things to do differently in the next workshop • Schedule the fourth workshop and discuss the 90-Day Team Operating System process you will use going forward • Review/commit to all Work Agreements • Acknowledgments & appreciations		

Reminders for the Third RMT Workshop

The third RMT workshop's outcome focuses on teammate growth and development.

There are many developmental topics to choose from; several are discussed in RMT's book, *Right-Minded Teamwork in Any Team: The Ultimate Team Building Method to Create a Team That Works as One.*

See the section Ele*ment #5 - Right-Minded Teammates: Strengthen Performance* for more details.

The third workshop agenda template you just saw uses one of RMT's Team-Building Exercises, called the **About Me & My Preferences** team-building exercise. Instructions are below but can also be found in the above mentioned book.

Please note:
- At the end of the second workshop, teammates brainstorm a list of potential teammate development topics to address in their third workshop.

  Whether or not the team decides on the development topic then or later, a decision will be made approximately two weeks before the third workshop. Doing so will give everyone enough time to prepare.

- RMT also recommends that when your team starts meeting every 90 days, every third workshop should be devoted to teammate growth and development.

About Me & My Preferences
Team-Building Exercise

The Goal

The goal of this real-world **About Me & My Preferences** Team-Building Exercise is to increase teammates' understanding of each other's work preferences.

RMT has facilitated this exercise many times. It has been wildly successful. And it is much faster than conducting a personality-type-style workshop.

It is more effective than personality workshops in most cases because teammates address their most important work preferences. Doing that means they create meaningful **Work Agreements** to build and sustain Right-Minded Teamwork.

Do this exercise, and you will be following Right-Minded Teamwork's philosophy of "do no harm, and work as one."

Exercise Instructions

- Teammates choose one, maybe two, of the questions below to answer.
- They bring their answers to a team-building workshop.
- Each teammate shares at least one answer.
- Other teammates ask clarifying questions.
- If appropriate, the team or individual teammates will create Work Agreements to resolve identified challenges.
- IMPORTANT: Conduct this conversation in a collaborative and compassionate spirit. Find ways to work with another's preferences. Do not try to change another teammate.
- Remember: Right-Minded Teammates do no harm as they work as one.

Preferences Exercise Questions

1. How would you describe your work style? What works or does not work well when it comes to interacting with you and your work style?
2. If another teammate thinks you are about to make a mistake, what is the best way for them to respond or call it to your attention? And what will be your responsibility?
3. What is the best way for others to express disagreement or alternative opinions without offending you? And what will be your responsibility if they don't?
4. What are your pet peeves? What makes you mad? If you are triggered, what is the best way for you and the other person to recover?
5. The biggest mistake another teammate can make with me is _____, and the best way we can recover is _____.
6. The best way to communicate with me is _____, and the best way to motivate me is _____.

90-Day Operating Plan - Ongoing

Approximately 90 days after your third workshop (and every 90 days after that), your team will follow your Team Operating Plan (created in the second workshop).

Approximately two weeks before your 90-day workshop, the team will conduct another *Team Performance Factor Assessment*, and then the team meets to assess progress, identify opportunities, take action, and achieve new teamwork improvements.

The team will repeat this process every 90-days.

Note: These quarterly meetings are designed to meet your team's specific need in achieving and sustaining your version of Right-Minded Teamwork.

They almost guarantee you stay focused on your goals, doing the right things right to achieve 100% customer satisfaction.

RMT's only guidance on how to design your quarterly agendas is to:
- Use the *Team Performance Factor Assessment* to identify your next 90-day goals, and
- Conduct a teammate growth and development workshop every third quarter.

	TMS: 90-Day Team-Building Workshop Date: Time: Location:
Attendees	List all teammates
Please Read	Complete our *Team Performance Factor Assessment* and turn into the team leader by ____
Please Bring	your Performance Factor Assessment answers

Purpose & Desired Outcomes

Purpose: Create and sustain our version of Right-Minded Teamwork

Desired Outcomes

1. Discuss and agree on our team's actual performance during the previous 90 days
2. Discuss the current *Team Performance Factor Assessment* results
3. Discuss and agree on two to three improvement opportunities for the next 90 days
4. Create an improvement action plan for those opportunities

Agenda		
What	Who	When
Welcome & Kick-Off • Share purpose, the desired outcome • Review agenda, meeting behavior, agreements	Team Leader, Facilitator	10-15 min
Last Quarter – 90-Day Results • Discuss and agree on our team's actual results • Create a Report of Improvement to be submitted to our team's sponsor		
Next Quarter – 90-Day Plan • Discuss our current *Team Performance Factor Assessment* results • List all potential improvement opportunities. • Discuss and agree on two or three opportunities for the next 90 days • Create an improvement action plan for those opportunities		
Closure • List workshop positives as well as things to do differently in the next workshop • Schedule the next 90-day Team Operating Plan meeting date • Review/commit to all Work Agreements and Action Plans • Acknowledgments & appreciations		

Report of Improvement Template

Our Goal or Outcome	
Information Start Date End Date Team Leader Teammates	
What Was Done	
Actual Improvement or Results Measurable Non-Measurable	
Cost of Improvement Measurable Non-Measurable	
Suggestions for Future Projects or Outcomes	
Acknowledgment of Contributions	

10 Steps: How to Facilitate Team Work Agreements

Overview

Work Agreements are the third Element of Right-Minded Teamwork's 5 Elements framework. They are used to transform unproductive, dysfunctional behavior into positive and constructive work behavior.

The 10 Steps involved in creating Work Agreements are outlined in the book *How to Facilitate Team Work Agreements: A Practical, 10-Step Process for Building a Right-Minded Team That Works as One.*

That book is written primarily for team facilitators, and your TMS facilitators will learn this skill. But leaders and teammates can easily follow along to build Work Agreements, too. In this section, we'll introduce this powerful, team-building tool.

What Are Work Agreements?

Work Agreements are team covenants or vows that transform teammates' dysfunctional and non-productive behavior into team cohesiveness and accomplishment.

Work Agreements are not guidelines or ground rules. They are emotionally mature promises that guide a team to work collaboratively towards the shared goal of achieving customer satisfaction.

> *If you've ever been part of a team, you know it is not a matter of if conflict will occur among teammates. It is a question of when.*

A team without Work Agreements is like a machine without an operator's manual. Teammates may function at acceptable levels for a while, but eventually, they will decline into separateness and self-interest.

It is far better to have Work Agreements in place before teammate disagreements happen. Established Work Agreements can serve to mitigate and even make positive use of those clashes when they occur. However, even if your team is already in conflict, it's still not too late (and will never be!) to create and live team Work Agreements.

To create Work Agreements, leaders and teammates must openly discuss unresolved interpersonal or work process issues and together agree on what acceptable behavior looks like going forward. Emotionally mature and productive teammates intentionally create Work Agreements because they have experienced the benefits of a unified team with shared interests and common goals.

In my 35 years of active team building, I facilitated over 500 teams around the globe, many of them beautifully diverse and multicultural.

Every single team created Work Agreements and succeeded as a result.

Work Agreements work when teammates live them.

The process for facilitating Work Agreements is not complicated. Nonetheless, becoming proficient in facilitating their creation takes dedication and a willingness to learn. As you practice, you will make mistakes, especially in the beginning. Don't give up. Your mistakes will not hurt your teams - I promise. The long-lasting benefits you will bring to the team as you improve your facilitation skills will far outweigh any initial missteps.

By following the steps in the book ***How to Facilitate Team Work Agreements****: A Practical, 10-Step Process for Building a Right-Minded Team That Works as One*, you can learn how to facilitate Work Agreements for your team.

Facilitating Work Agreements –
A Narrative Description of the Process

To introduce you to the Work Agreements process, below is a narrative description of the 10 Steps. The 10 Steps book also includes a graphic illustration of the workshop flipcharts and more in-depth, detailed descriptions and guidance for each of the Steps.

Let's start by assuming you and the team leader have conducted the orientation meeting.

Preparation Steps 1-3

Take these steps before the workshop.

1. In the orientation meeting, the team agreed on the first teamwork topic(s) to address.
2. Determine the topic's desired outcome.
3. Design an opening question to be asked to kick off the topic dialogue.

In **Step 1**, the team leader informs the facilitator what they want to achieve and why.

Often, some difficult situation has occurred that has precipitated the desire for this workshop. After you understand the leader's desired teamwork outcomes, you interview all teammates to more thoroughly understand what they want to achieve and why.

After the teammate interviews, you share the team's collective input with the leader, which finalizes the first few topics to be addressed in the first workshop.

In the book, we use two outcomes as teaching examples: improving communication and team decision-making. The first is a behavioral issue, and the second is a work process issue.

In **Step 2**, the facilitator and leader finalize the agenda that includes the desired outcomes.

In **Step 3**, the facilitator creates an opening question for the chosen topics. We will use improved communication in this narrative. In the workshop, the facilitator asks the opening question to launch a team discussion. Eventually, this discussion leads to Work Agreements.

Facilitation Steps 4-10

4. When the time is right, ask the opening question.
5. Capture legitimate behavioral answers on a flipchart.
6. Write and propose an intention statement.
7. After a short dialogue, ask if teammates agree to live the intention.
8. Write clarifications and conditions for acceptance.
9. Create an interlocking accountability condition.
10. When everyone approves the Work Agreement, celebrate. Move to the next topic.

The Workshop

Imagine you are 10 minutes into your workshop. The team leader has welcomed everyone. All teammates have agreed to the desired outcomes, agenda, ground rules, and the day's logistics.

Before you ask your opening question, take five minutes to introduce the **Right Choice Model**. Your goal is to present the Model in such a way that when you finish teaching it, all teammates declare,

> *Of course, we need to approach* [our issue] *in a Right-Minded, accountable way. Let's get started.*

Another option is the team leader could present the Right Choice Model by relating it to a current difficult team challenge.

Either way, after you present it and the team has collectively committed, it is the right time for you to ask the opening question.

To learn more about the Right Choice Model and how to apply it to your team, go to the section below: *What is the Right Choice Model?* Or go to RightMindedTeamwork.com or your favorite book retailer, and pick up ***How to Apply the Right Choice Model***: *Create a Right-Minded Team That Works as One*. Within the book, look for the section titled, "How to Present & Apply the Right Choice Model in Your Team." There, you will be given specific instructions on how to present the Right Choice Model successfully, including how to relate it to your team's current challenge.

When you, as the facilitator, ask the opening question, you have officially started the team's honest discussion on the first teamwork topic - **Step 4.** Here is a good opening question:

If we communicated respectfully, what would you see or hear teammates say or do, or not say or do?

Up to this point, you have been doing most of the talking. After asking the opening question, you move into listening, observing, and facilitating.

Now that the opening question has been asked, you listen to the team's discussion, which may last 30-60 minutes. All the while, you are capturing legitimate behavioral answers on a flipchart - **Step 5**.

In **Step 6**, while teammates continue discussing their topic, you think about and write an intention statement. The proposed statement should evolve from the team's list of answers. When the time is right, you suggest the intention statement. Here is an example:

Each teammate will communicate in a respectful way with each other and our customers.

In **Step 7**, you ask teammates if they will agree to live the proposed intention. Most of the time, teammates agree. But they usually believe it needs more work. It is still a work in progress.

In **Step 8**, the team discusses their specific clarifications or conditions for acceptance of the intention statement. As teammates add and edit their conditions, you and the team leader periodically ask them, if they truly lived their Work-Agreement-in-progress, would they achieve their desired outcome? Most of the time, they will say yes. This "yes" motivates the team to continue making the "right" Agreement for this team.

Finally, **Step 9** calls for "interlocking accountability" within the Work Agreement, a vital step to encouraging the team to live their Agreements day in and day out. Fortunately, you will only need to create interlocking accountability once. It will apply to all Work Agreements.

In the *Real Team Work Agreements* section below, you will find a real example of interlocking accountability. Look at the final condition in the behavioral Communication Agreement.

In **Step 10**, every teammate publicly commits to hold themselves and others accountable to upholding the team Work Agreement. At this point, everyone should all genuinely believe the Agreement will help the team achieve its goals.

It's important to note that it's not unusual for people to break their Work Agreements after the workshop. Often, this breach is just an honest mistake or a habit not yet transformed. However, if a teammate continues to break a Work Agreement, the team should have an agreed-upon condition (Step 9's interlocking accountability) that clarifies how they will confront one another.

Two Types of Work Agreements

Work Agreements may be process-driven or behavior-driven.

A **process Work Agreement** describes who will do what task and which work method they will use. It defines work tasks in terms of roles, responsibilities, interfaces, or procedures.

A **behavioral Work Agreement** describes how people will behave while performing tasks, such as the ways teammates will bring to light, communicate, and resolve difficult performance issues or teammate conflicts. This type of Work Agreement aims for transparency in all interpersonal interactions.

A Work Agreement that is wholeheartedly agreed upon includes an intention statement that defines your team's choice followed by clarifications or conditions for acceptance.

Below you will find two real examples. The first one is a behavioral team Communication Work Agreement. The other is a process, a Decision-Making Work Agreement.

I worked with these teams for a few years. With my guidance, it took this 10-person team about four hours to create these two Work Agreements.

They were phenomenally successful Agreements because teammates passionately created and actively lived them day in and day out.

Real Team Work Agreements

Behavioral Agreement – Communication

Team Choice: Intention Statement
1. Each teammate will communicate in a respectful way.

Clarifications / Conditions for Acceptance:

A. We will use good communication techniques that include appropriate body language and tone of voice, plus suitable words.
B. If we see or hear disrespect or we hear an inappropriate behind-the-back conversation, we own it and need to step in.
C. If someone unintentionally shows disrespect, we will give them the benefit of the doubt, let them know, and create a new way to interact going forward.
D. We will actively support team decisions in word, deed, and energy; we will use our decision-making protocol agreement for key decisions.
E. We will be on time for meetings.
F. We will ask, "May I interrupt you?"
G. We will use observable facts during disagreements and decision-making, and we will acknowledge when we are using assumptions.
H. We will understand each other's roles, ask for help if we need it, share relevant information and if helpful, give constructive feedback in private.
I. If someone continues to break this agreement, we will tell them that we will invite a third party to help if there is continued disagreement. If that doesn't solve the issues, we will all go to a higher authority for support and resolution.

Process Agreement – Decision-Making Protocol

Team Choice: Intention Statement
2. We will go for consensus for all key team decisions, but our fallback will be that Maria [team leader] will decide if we cannot reach a consensus.

Conditions for Acceptance / Clarification

A. Before entering a discussion, we'll agree on the decision-making method and fall back, plus when [date] a decision will be made.
B. Before delving into a solution, we will create an opportunity or problem statement.
C. At the beginning of our discussion, we will determine boundaries & givens (i.e., time sensitivity; cost, hassle, impact, 80% or 100% perfect decision, etc.).
D. We provide a business case (appropriate justification) for our decision, including cost/benefit.
E. During our conversations, we will advocate and inquire. We will not hold back. For instance, we will acknowledge assumptions and facts.
F. To create the best solutions, we will also think about alternative ways to test our solution (Devil's Advocate).
G. If we find ourselves at an impasse, we will call a "time out" to calm down or acquire more technical information.
H. When a decision is made, we will accurately represent and support the decision.
I. We do this agreement because we want to improve teamwork and trust in one another.
J. We will hold ourselves and others accountable for living the letter and the spirit of this agreement; we will fine-tune it as necessary

Onboarding New Teammates

When a new person, leader, or teammate, joins your team, it is vitally important to properly onboard them within their first week on the job. In a single, short meeting where everyone attends, the onboarding is easily and effectively accomplished.

First, you present all your RMT goals and Work Agreements along with why they were created. Next, you invite the new teammate to ask clarifying questions. Afterward, you ask them to accept the team's goals and actively live the team's Work Agreements.

12 Steps: Design a Right-Minded, Team-Building Workshop

Overview

Right-Minded Teamwork does not advocate team games, outdoor exercises, or social events as legitimate substitutes for team building. They can be fun, but they are indirect and do not resolve a team's real issues.

Right-Minded Teamwork is not a game-based or social approach to team building. It is a "real-world" method that actually works.

The RMT book, *Design a Right-Minded, Team-Building Workshop*, will teach your TMS RMT facilitators how to design a practical, real-world, team-building workshop. Your RMT Facilitator Training Team will teach this method to internal and perhaps even external facilitators. Though the 12 Steps book is written primarily for team facilitators, leaders and teammates can also easily follow the Steps to design a successful team workshop.

Below you will find a short, narrative description of the 12 Steps. Full details and guidance can be found in the book.

How to Design a
Right-Minded
TEAMWORK
Team-Building Workshop:
12-Step Process

Overview: 12 Steps, Three Phases

The RMT process includes 12 steps presented in three phases:

Contract: Designing the workshop (Steps 1-9)

Commence: Facilitating the workshop (Step 10)

Carry On: Keeping up momentum after the workshop (Steps 11-12)

Contract: Designing the Workshop (Steps 1-9)

Step 1

To begin, the team leader determines the workshop's purpose. Usually, workshops focus on something the team needs to change or improve because teammates are not working together as one.

Step 2

The leader conveys the purpose and potential outcomes of the workshop to the facilitator. Both agree to follow the 12 Steps process to design the workshop.

Step 3

The leader gives the facilitator permission to think of their initial desired outcomes as symptoms, allowing the facilitator to uncover root causes the leader may not have considered. It's not unusual between steps 3 and 7 to learn that what the leader said they initially wanted may not be what the team needs.

Step 4

The facilitator creates and presents a 1st Draft Plan to the leader. The plan includes the initial set of workshop outcomes, agenda, Punch List of workshop topics, and a workshop announcement plan.

Step 5

The leader announces the workshop and prepares teammates. Teammates learn the facilitator will interview them. By offering their input and perspective, teammates will eagerly participate in designing the workshop outcomes and agenda.

Step 6

The facilitator conducts a Right-Minded Teammate survey to help identify potential workshop outcomes.

Step 7

The facilitator interviews all teammates, summarizing their collective views in the Punch List document.

Step 8

The facilitator creates and presents a 2nd Draft Plan to the leader.

Step 9

The leader and facilitator fine-tune and agree on the final outcomes and workshop agenda. Together, they distribute the agenda and begin preparing teammates for the workshop.

Commence: Facilitating the Workshop (Step 10)

Step 10

The leader and facilitator conduct the workshop and achieve workshop outcomes.

Teammates agree to track their performance after the workshop. They agree on what they will track, how they will track it, and to whom they will report their progress. They agree to conduct team-building workshops every 90 days.

Carry On: Keeping Up Momentum (Steps 11-12)

Step 11

For the next 90 days, the team implements their tasks and tracks their progress.

Step 12

The leader and facilitator either begin designing the second workshop or transfer that responsibility to others.

Every 90 days, the cycle continues onward, beginning with Step 1 again.

As this cycle is repeated over time, the team grows and evolves into a team that consistently works as one.

30 Right-Minded Teamwork
Attitudes & Behaviors

Over decades of team-building work, I worked with hundreds of teams. Along the way, I collected their Right-Minded attitudes and behaviors into a list of choices that I grouped into **work behaviors** and **work processes.**

Were You Born With These Thoughts & Attitudes?

Thoughts and attitudes always precede teamwork behavior.

Right-Minded attitudes come from Reason. Wrong-minded attitudes come from Ego.

The good news is that Right-Minded attitudes are natural. They are already inside you and your teammates.

When you think about any of the wrong-minded Ego attitudes listed below, ask yourself,

> *Was I born with these depressing, debilitating, and awful attitudes?*

Your answer will always be **"no!"**

You learned those wrong-minded attitudes from Ego. That means *you can unlearn them, too.* Right-Minded Teamwork will show you how.

You *Can* Change Your Mind

In 35 years of team-building facilitation, I heard too many well-intentioned albeit wrong-minded teammates say,

That's just the way I am. I can't change.

That is **simply not true**.

What is true is that they refused to change their minds.

When someone says they cannot change, what they are really saying is their behavior is more powerful than their mind.

When they realize and joyfully accept that **their mind is in charge**, they have opened the way for happiness, inner peace, and Right-Minded Teamwork **Thinking**.

The 30 Right-Minded Teamwork Attitudes & Behaviors found on the next page will help your team and organization change your perspective and achieve Right-Minded Teamwork. Use this list to either adopt or adapt as your team's psychological goals and Work Agreements.

Work Behavior Attitudes

As the Decision-Maker, You Behave One Way or the Other!

EGO   DECISION MAKER   REASON

Demonstrate adversarial competition and power struggles	Demonstrate collaborative competition and synergy
Demonstrate victim or victimizer attitudes & behaviors	Exhibit accountable and responsible attitudes & behavior
Worry that "I am my mistakes;" continue to obsess over mistakes	Embrace that "I am not my mistakes;" mistakes are opportunities for me to learn
Noticeable lack of emotional maturity and empathy	Desire to be emotionally mature and compassionate
Exhibit self-centered attitudes	Exhibit we-centered attitudes
Hold & project grievances; Never forget or forgive	Embrace & extend forgiveness; Let go of issues from the past
After mistakes, helplessness occurs, and I choose to give up or not try as hard	After mistakes, forgiveness occurs, and I choose to try again and again

Work Behavior Attitudes (Continued)

There's a mindset of scarcity, a belief that to give is to lose	There's an attitude of abundance, a belief that to give is to receive
There is suspicion, closed-mindedness, and resistance to change	There is readiness and open-mindedness for positive change
Too often, people restate their position, believing they are right, and others are wrong	We always seek mutual understanding: believing together, we are right
I believe I'm the smartest, and I can prove it	We believe none of us is as smart as all of us
I demonstrate a conscious or unconscious attitude of confusion, chaos, complexity, and drama	We continually demonstrate a conscious attitude of clarity, order, simplicity, and calmness
There's a widespread belief that difficult team situations and changes determine how we feel	We know for sure that our minds determine how we feel about difficult situations or changes
We believe it is best to keep quiet when correction is needed	We have a team culture of appropriately speaking up when a correction is needed
We believe in these attitudes: vulnerability, unkindness, hate, attack, blame	We embrace these attitudes: invulnerability, love, kindness, do no harm, work as one

Work Behavior Attitudes (Continued)

We believe in power over others	We believe in power with others
Growth is painful; remember, if there is no pain, there is no gain	Growth doesn't have to be painful; learning is joyously attained and gladly remembered
It is best to do unto others (reject, attack, defend) before they do unto you	We do unto others (accept, forgive, adjust) as we would have them do unto us
There is a feeling of avoidance and criticism among teammates	There is a spirit of acknowledgment and reward among teammates
There is a love and a need for power, fame, money, and pleasure	We strive for non-attachment to power, fame, money, and pleasure
Our team is a battleground where conflict is prolonged as we act like victims or victimizers	Our team is our learning classroom where conflict is resolved as we act like Right-Minded Teammates
There is mistrust, fear, and lack of safety among teammates	There is trust, peace, and safety among teammates
Defensiveness is prevalent in our team	Defenselessness is widespread in our team

Process Behavior Attitudes

Your Team Can Operate One Way or the Other!

The team's purpose, vision, and mission are unclear and not supported	Our team continuously clarifies our purpose, vision, and mission and actively support them
There is no discernable team operating system	There is an efficient, continuous improvement team operating system in place
There is a predominant attitude of avoidance and complaining	We have an attitude and a system for acknowledgment and reward
Disagreements and a lack of clear roles and responsibilities exist	We periodically clarify teammate roles and responsibilities
We are unclear who makes decisions and how	Our team has a clear and effective decision-making Work Agreement
We spend too much time and energy applying inefficient work processes	Our work processes and procedures are clear, understood, accepted, and efficient
Too often, people are punished for making mistakes	We always embrace an attitude of converting mistakes into learning opportunities

Actionable Attitudes = Better Behaviors

The Right-Minded attitudes in these charts are practical. However, these noble thoughts and attitudes will do no good unless you discuss them and define what they mean for your team.

Once you have identified and defined the behaviors associated with your chosen attitudes, captured in your team Work Agreements, you must also make the conscious choice to live them going forward.

Don't let your team's insignificant, Ego-driven squabbles pull you down. Be vigilant and demonstrate by your actions and behaviors that you have risen above your old, petty, teamwork battleground issues.

Be vigilant and demonstrate by your actions and behaviors that you have risen above your old, petty, teamwork battleground issues.

No team situation can pull you into Ego's realm of conflict when you believe it is far better to collaborate and win than argue and lose.

Remember, it is from your collective Right Mind that you create your Work Agreements. And when you make and follow your promises, you are uniting with each other without the Ego. When you do that, you have returned to the United Circle of Right-Minded Thinking. From that unified circle, it will be much easier to recover from any difficult team situation because you have, at that moment, restored your team's collective Right Mind to Reason.

What Is the Right Choice Model?

The Right Choice Model is a tool to help you and your teammates make the conscious choice to follow *your team's* "do no harm, work as one" attitudes and behaviors.

The Model is available in a 3x4 inch card, perfect for printing and distributing to teammates, and an 8x11 inch poster. It consists of two parts.

The first part contains two loops. The upper loop describes Right-Minded Accountability, and the lower loop defines victimization.

The other part presents the Right-Minded Accountability definition plus the important Right-Minded question that moves you and your teammates back into your right minds.

Right Choice promotes the concept that every person has free will. Free will means you are 100% responsible for how you respond to every situation, circumstance, and event that happens.

When difficult team situations occur, you either:

Act as an ally, choosing to demonstrate accountable, responsible, and Right-Minded behaviors

Choose to be adversarial, reacting to the difficult situation by becoming a victim or victimizer and demonstrating wrong-minded behaviors

Wrong choices lead to victimization, blame, and punishment among teammates. They guarantee solutions are not found because teammates are too busy pointing fingers at others and defending themselves.

Right-Minded choices are the only sane response to challenging team situations.

Why?

 Because teammates who demonstrate the Right actions and behaviors find real solutions to their problems.

The End: Begin Your TMS Journey

Deploying Right-Minded Teamwork is a transformational journey. It will become known as one of the most profitable cultural changes you and your organization have ever made. The benefits of a well-managed TMS far exceed the challenges of establishing it and seeing it through the first two years of operation.

When your TMS evolves into a standard and expected practice, just like your employee performance management program, your organization will have clear evidence that RMT's Team Management System benefits you and your organization's customers. You'll likely wonder why your organization never created a TMS before.

As you begin your journey, return to this book frequently for guidance and direction. Keep going even when things feel tough. And remember, you are never alone. I am here to support you on your Right-Minded path.

The End

Thanks for reading our Right-Minded Teamwork book, *Achieve Your Organization's Strategic Plan: Create a Right-Minded Team Management System to Ensure All Teams Work as One.* If you enjoyed it, won't you please take a moment to leave a review at your favorite retailer or RightMindedTeamwork.com?

Also, in a few pages, you will find something beneficial: a *Glossary of Right-Minded Teamwork Terms and Resources.*

And finally, on behalf of Reason and all the Right-Minded Teammates around the world, we extend our best wishes to you and your organization as you create another *Right-Minded Team and organization that Works Together as One.*

DECISION MAKER

REASON

About the Author

The idea of "developing people and teams that work" began as a company statement for organizational consulting firm Lord & Hogan LLC, founded in 1990. Leveraging his personable but results-oriented consulting style, founder **Dan Hogan** devoted his career to transforming dysfunctional work relationships into positive, supportive bonds.

But over the course of his 40-year career, something shifted.

Through his work as an organizational development coach, performance consultant, and Certified Master Facilitator, the mission of Lord & Hogan also became Dan's own.

Better Work Relationships = Stronger, More Productive Teams

As a consultant and facilitator, Dan advocated for the individuals and managed teams he served. He emphasized the equal importance of strong team member relationships and solid business systems and processes to overall business success. His efforts spoke for themselves as his clients began to notice results.

With Dan's guidance, teams were more productive almost overnight. There were fewer day-to-day interpersonal issues. Project management efforts were finally back on track. Teams were achieving their goals.

After being stuck for so long, these teams were moving forward... smoothly. As one client said, "Dan has the unique ability to hear the confusion and bring clarity. He has helped me, our team, and our organization to move to the next level."

The Right-Minded Teamwork Model: A Legacy

Not only did Dan's efforts deliver consistent, powerful results (gaining him many long-term clients over the years) at a higher level, his work also positively impacted the practice of behavioral change management.

Over the course of his career, Dan refined his ideas along with the help of his clients and the teams he served. Eventually, he created his own proprietary tools, processes, and strategies. Of all his models and creations, Dan's most significant accomplishment has been the development of his Right-Minded Teamwork model, which perfectly assembles all his tools and processes into a single, streamlined approach.

At its core, Right-Minded Teamwork (RMT) is a continuous improvement loop for small and large groups; it has been proven to work with teams of all sizes. No matter what team challenges or interpersonal issues are happening, RMT has the power to correct them.

By first bringing the team together under a unified set of goals, then providing tools for teams to explore, understand, and work through their underlying concerns, Right-Minded Teamwork provides teams with the opportunity to address unproductive behaviors in a safe, non-condemning way. Focusing on acceptance, forgiveness, and self-adjustment among teammates, Right-Minded Teamwork directly addresses and resolves the root cause of even the most difficult teamwork situations.

After directly serving over 500 teams in seven countries and creating lasting tools and resources that will go on to support countless additional teams, leaders, and facilitators on every continent, Dan Hogan has left a legacy to be proud of. No longer an active facilitator, Dan has transformed his ideas and contributions into powerful, effective, team-building tools available online, providing team facilitators and team leaders around the globe access to Right-Minded Teamwork.

Books by Dan Hogan

Reason, Ego & the Right-Minded Teamwork Myth: The Philosophy and Process for Creating a Right-Minded Team That Works Together as One

This book explores two foundational concepts: the Right-Minded Teamwork Myth, a short tale that presents RMT's underlying teamwork philosophy, and the Right-Minded Teamwork team-building process, a step-by-step approach to implementing RMT in any team.

Right-Minded Teamwork in Any Team: The Ultimate Team-Building Method to Create a Team That Works as One

Right-Minded Teamwork is built on a framework of 5 Elements, explored in this book. These two goals and three methods are implemented into your team through three team-building workshops conducted over a six-to-12-month period. Once your team completes their third workshop, you move into a 90-day, continuous improvement operating plan that allows your team to achieve their goals, do no harm and work together as one.

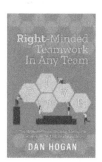

How to Facilitate Team Work Agreements*: A Practical, 10-Step Process for Building a Right-Minded Team That Works as One*

Team Work Agreements are collective pledges made by your team to transform non-productive or dysfunctional actions into positive and constructive work behavior. Though this book is written primarily for team facilitators, team leaders and teammates may also follow these steps to create powerful, effective Work Agreements to solve and prevent interpersonal and process problems.

How to Apply the Right Choice Model*: Create a Right-Minded Team That Works as One*

The concept of Right Choice states every person has free will. Free will means you are 100% responsible for how you respond to every situation, circumstance, and event. When difficult team problems occur, you either act as an ally or an adversary. When you choose to be an ally, you demonstrate positive, accountable behavior. When you are an adversary, you behave as either a victim or a victimizer. This book and model will guide you through creating a team of productive, supportive, Right-Minded teammate allies.

7 *Mindfulness Training Lessons*: Improve Teammates' Ability to Work as One with Right-Minded Thinking

If you want your team working together as one, you want them thinking as one, too. These 7 Mindfulness Training Lessons will help you achieve a positive team mindset by guiding teammates to raise their awareness of thoughts, choices, and behaviors. Teammates may also use these lessons to create the team's Right-Minded thought system. The 7 Lessons can be summed up in one sentence, emphasizing three words: Right-Minded Teammates **accept**, **forgive**, and **adjust** their thinking and work behavior. When teammates follow these lessons, they **do no harm** while **working together as one.**

Right-Minded Teamwork: 9 Right Choices for Building a Team That Works as One

This quick read is an excellent Right-Minded Teamwork primer and a terrific way to introduce RMT to teammates. These nine teamwork choices are universal, self-evident, and self-validating. You want them in your team. In this book, each of the 9 Right Choices is defined, and exercises are provided for applying each choice.

Design a Right-Minded, Team-Building Workshop: *12 Steps to Create a Team That Works as One*

This book includes complete instruction on how to design a practical, real-world, team-building workshop that teammates actually want to attend. Unlike many team activities labeled "team building" that are really more "team bonding," true team-building workshops are intentionally designed to solve a team's real-world problems. Written primarily for team facilitators, team leaders and teammates may also follow these 12 steps to design an effective, transformative team workshop.

Achieve Your Organization's Strategic Plan: *Create a Right-Minded Team Management System to Ensure All Teams Work as One*

When a single team within an organization works together as one, they are effective and productive. When an enterprise works with the same level of synergy, it is exponentially more powerful. A Team Management System like the Right-Minded Teamwork TMS model taught in this book lays the groundwork for your organization to get every team on the same page. By following RMT's four-part rollout plan, you can create and deploy your own Team Management System, align teammate attitudes, and work behavior with company values, and bring your entire organization together to work as one and achieve your strategic plan.

Find Dan Hogan & Right-Minded Teamwork Online

Visit my website: https://rightmindedteamwork.com

Subscribe to my blog: Teamwork News:
https://rightmindedteamwork.com/blog

Friend me on LinkedIn:
https://www.linkedin.com/company/rightminded-teamwork

Follow me on Facebook:
https://www.facebook.com/RightMindedTeamwork

Favorite my Smashwords Author Page:
https://www.smashwords.com/profile/view/rightmindedteamwork

Read my Smashwords Interview:
https://www.smashwords.com/interview/rightmindedteamwork

Follow me on Amazon Author Page: https://amzn.to/3noStKA

Glossary of
Right-Minded Teamwork
Terms & Resources

100% Customer Satisfaction

Creating 100% customer satisfaction is a primary goal of Right-Minded Teamwork. Your team is responsible for providing quality products and services to customers; for your team and enterprise to succeed, your customers deserve to be 100% satisfied.

With a strong customer satisfaction plan, as described in *Right-Minded Teamwork in Any Team*, your teammates will strive to achieve customer satisfaction while consistently achieving other business goals.

7 Mindfulness Training Lessons

Achieving Right-Minded Teamwork involves adopting an attitude of mindfulness. The *7 Mindfulness Training Lessons* teach you to think in a Right-Minded way, ensuring you **do no harm** as you **work as one** with your teammates.

These powerful lessons are summed up in one sentence, with emphasis on three words:

*Right-Minded Teammates **accept**, **forgive**, and **adjust** their thinking and work behavior.*

In every circumstance, especially during difficult team situations, Right-Minded Teammates practice mindfulness to move them from defensiveness and blame into a Right-Minded, allied way of thinking and behaving.

Inspired by *A Course in Miracles* and our Right Choice Model, the *7 Mindfulness Training Lessons* is a teaching tool designed to help those willing to apply them to ensure they return to the Unified Circle of Right-Minded Thinking.

Go to RightMindedTeamwork.com or visit your favorite book retailer to pick up your copy of ***7 Mindfulness Training Lessons***: *Improve Teammates' Ability to Work as One with Right-Minded Thinking.*

10 Characteristics of Right-Minded Teammates

Right-Minded Teammates have many different surface traits and personalities. They are not all alike. They have numerous backgrounds, vastly different experiences, and a wide range of skills.

Nevertheless, it is understood that the Right-Minded Teammate, in their own particular behavioral style, happily live these characteristics because they align the teammate's authentic *self* with their team's version of the RMT motto: *do no harm, work as one,* and *none of us is as smart as all of us.*

You will find a complete description of these characteristics in RMT's book: *Right-Minded Teamwork in Any Team: The Ultimate Team Building Method to Create a Team That Works as One.*

1. Trust	2. Honesty	3. Tolerance
4. Gentleness	5. Joy	6. Defenselessness
7. Generosity	8. Patience	9. Open-Mindedness
	10. Faithfulness	

12 Steps Workshop Design Process

Design a Right-Minded, Team-Building Workshop:12 Steps to Create a Team That Works as One. This book will teach you how to design a practical, real-world team-building workshop.

The 12 steps are grouped into three phases: Contract, Commence, and Carry on. Written primarily for team facilitators, team leaders, and teammates can easily follow the steps to design a successful team-building workshop. Because this method engages teammates in designing the agenda, it virtually guarantees that teammates *cannot wait* to attend the workshop. They *know* that they will get real work done in a safe, "no harm" environment when they meet.

A Course in Miracles

Oneness. Forgiveness is the key to happiness, inner peace, undifferentiated unity, and ultimately – *oneness*. "A Course In Miracles (ACIM) is a unique spiritual self-study program designed to awaken us to the truth of our *oneness* with God and Love," as posted on ACIM.org and ACIM.org/ACIM/en. See the Foundation for A Course in Miracles at FACIM.org, where Ken Wapnick, the founder, created this beautiful definition.

A Course in Miracles is a psychological approach to spirituality where forgiveness is the central theme, and inner peace is the result.

ACIM and other moral and spiritual philosophies that advocate and help people everywhere **work together as One** has inspired Right-Minded Teamwork. We used Ken's definition as a guide to create the Right-Minded Teamwork definition.

Right-Minded Teamwork is a business-oriented, psychological approach to team building where acceptance, forgiveness, and adjustments are teammate characteristics, and 100% customer satisfaction is the team's result.

All Right-Minded Teamwork methods, processes, and tools seamlessly work together to help you create and sustain a *Team That Works Together as **One.***

Accept, Forgive, Adjust

These three terms are at the core of Right-Minded Teammate Attitudes & Behaviors. These verbs are also central to the *7 Mindfulness Training Lessons*, which are summed up in the sentence, *Right-Minded Teammates **accept**, **forgive**, and **adjust** their thinking and work behavior.*

Furthermore, these three concepts are included in the definition of Right-Minded Teamwork:

*Right-Minded Teamwork is a business-oriented, psychological approach to team building where **acceptance**, **forgiveness**, and **adjustment** are teammate characteristics, and 100% customer satisfaction is the team's result.*

Lastly, these terms are also incorporated as three of the five steps in the *Right Choice Model*, which describes accountable and responsible Right-Minded Teamwork behavior.

Ally or Adversary Teammate

Right-Minded Teamwork asserts that as teammates, you either work together as allies, or you pull apart, viewing each other as adversaries.

Allies work towards achieving team goals. Adversaries work towards individual elevation, which separates and divides the team.

To determine whether you are in an ally or adversary mindset, ask yourself, *Do I want to be right, or do I want our team to be successful?* Allies want to be part of a successful team. Adversaries want to be right, no matter the cost.

As an adversary, Ego persuades you to compete with your teammates. As an ally, Reason says the opposite. Reason gently reminds you that separateness prevents true success. There cannot be oneness or collaboration where there is competition.

As the Decision-Maker, you choose to follow either Reason or Ego. You either collaborate or compete. You are an ally or adversary. There is no middle ground.

If you choose to follow Reason and become an ally, you embrace and live your team's Work Agreements. If you decide to follow Ego, you become an adversary, creating a battleground inside yourself and your team.

To transform competitive adversaries into collaborative allies, start by following the *Right Choice Model*, creating team *Work Agreements*, and applying the *7 Mindfulness Training Lessons*.

Avoidance Behavior

Even though the term "avoidance behavior" is not often mentioned in the Right-Minded Teamwork model or books, avoidance behavior is easy to detect in teammates and RMT processes. If you notice it occurring, from an RMT perspective, you can consider it wrong-minded, adversarial behavior.

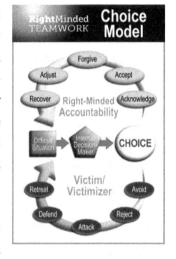

Identifying avoidance behaviors and attitudes and understanding the harm they cause is the first step in moving from a wrong-minded place into Right-Mindedness. The *7 Mindfulness Training Lessons* and the *Right Choice Model* are excellent tools for teaching yourself and your team how to act and behave in a Right-Minded, accountable way.

For example, if you look carefully at the *Right Choice Model's* lower loop, you will notice that the victim or victimizer first avoids the situation when a difficult situation occurs.

When Right-Minded Teammates ask themselves the *Right Choice Model* question, *How did I **create**, **promote**, or **allow** this difficult situation to happen?* they often realize they have unconsciously demonstrated avoidance behavior. Then, noticing their mistake, they simply choose to **accept, forgive,** and **adjust** their approach and return to living in accordance with their team *Work Agreements*.

Battleground:
Where People Are Punished for Mistakes

The battleground represents wrong-minded thinking. It is a mental attitude or thought system that defends and encourages adversarial behaviors such as blame and attack.

Think of the battleground as a psychological symbol for those moments when you realize you are listening to Ego, not Reason (like when you notice avoidance behavior). You recognize that you are having an Ego attack for whatever reason and have made a wrong-minded choice. When you are in the battleground, you "punish" others for their mistakes, either by victimizing others or becoming a victim yourself.

On the other hand, when you are in your right mind, you see your team as a lovely and safe classroom, the opposite of the battleground. You do not punish others. You choose, instead, to rise above the conflict.

The purpose of recognizing the battlegrounds in your mind is to own the pain that you are causing yourself which helps you recognize that you consciously want to leave it, overlook it, rise above it, and to transport your mind into the classroom where you return to the forgiving Unified Circle of Right-Minded Thinking with your teammates.

Right-Minded Teammates working in safe and supportive classrooms do not fight, blame, or punish. Instead, they choose oneness over separateness. They are committed to the team's success and achieving team goals.

To overcome a battleground in yourself or your team, go to RightMindedTeamwork.com, or visit your favorite book retailer to pick up your copy of *How to Apply the Right Choice Model: Create a Right-Minded Team That Works as One*. Inside, you will find a list of battleground attitudes and behaviors as well as the costs and benefits of classroom versus battleground thinking and behaving.

Certified Master Facilitator (CMF)

The Certified Master Facilitator (CMF) credential is a mark of excellence for facilitators. It is the highest available certification for facilitators. To learn more or to find a certified facilitator worldwide, visit the International Institute for Facilitation at INIFAC.org.

Classroom:
Where People Learn from Mistakes

Like the battleground, the classroom is a symbol. But unlike the battlefield, where people punish or are punished, the classroom is where you learn and find inspiration.

At some point in your past, you have experienced the joy and wonder of learning. Right-Minded Teamwork invites you to view your team as a safe place to experience this wonder and joy as you learn new teamwork skills and collaborate to achieve team goals.

When you are experiencing fear in any form or realize you are having an Ego attack, you are in the battleground. To return to the classroom, say to yourself, *There is nothing to fear. In my mind, I choose to rise above this silly battleground and head to my Right-Minded classroom. There, we are committed to do no harm and work as one. There, we will find solutions.*

By recognizing the fear behind your Ego attack and reminding yourself to return to the classroom, you experience a **moment of Reason**. You also strengthen your Right-Minded thought system and restore yourself to Right-Minded Thinking.

In the RMT book ***How to Apply the Right Choice Model****: Create a Right-Minded Team That Works as One,* you will find a list of 30 Right-Minded and wrong-minded attitudes and behaviors, plus the associated costs and benefits to your team.

Communication Work Agreement

What you think – *your thought system* – drives your communication in one of two ways. You either communicate as a collaborative ally or as a competitive, dysfunctional, and emotionally immature adversary.

Teams that work as one and achieve their goals regularly seek out opportunities to improve communication. They take positive action by creating and living a Communication Work Agreement that describes their team's agreed-upon communication style.

Right-Minded communication is a core concept in the book ***Right-Minded Teamwork****: 9 Right Choices for Building a Team That Works as One*, available at RightMindedTeamwork.com or your favorite book retailer.

To create your team's Communication Work Agreement, follow the suggestions in the book ***How to Facilitate Teamwork Agreements****: A Practical, 10-Step Process for Building a Right-Minded Team That Works as One*.

In there, you will find two real examples of which one is a team Communication Work Agreement.

Create, Promote, Allow

These three concepts form the foundation of the *Right Choice Model's* essential question:

*How have I **created**, **promoted**, or **allowed** this situation to occur?*

Asking and honestly answering this question ensures teammates are "owning their part" in a difficult situation.

These three concepts are also integrated into *7 **Mindful Training Lessons**: Improve Teammate's Ability to Work as One with Right-Minded Thinking.*

High-performing Right-Minded Teammates always ask themselves this question because it leads them to solutions. It is a clear demonstration of the RMT motto, "**Do no harm. Work as one.**"

Critical Few:
Complete Important Tasks First

When a team is stuck in the "full-plate syndrome," identifying and completing the critical few - those tasks that have the largest and most direct impact on the team's success - is key to moving forward.

At the root of the full-plate syndrome is the **team's collective fear**, driven by Ego, which declares you will get in trouble if you do not do it all... even though the truth is you can never do it all.

People who listen to Ego believe they do not have a choice. Rather than realistically prioritizing their workload, they punish themselves for failing to meet the unreasonable goal of completing everything. They drain their energy, lose their focus, and make mistakes. They become powerless, cynical, and burned out.

But Reason reminds us that we always have this choice:

We can either win by doing the critical few tasks, or we can lose by attempting to do everything.

Spend more time doing the right things right and let go of low-value tasks. Holding on to lower-value tasks is **not security**. It is **incarceration**.

The "critical few" concept is discussed in the book ***Right-Minded Teamwork****: 9 Right Choices for Building a Team That Works as One.*

See **Recognition: Make It Easy to Keep Going** for a related concept.

Decision-Maker: The Real You

Ken Wapnick, Ph.D., created the term "Decision-Maker" to define the "real you" in *A Course in Miracles*. For more on his work, visit FACIM.org.

DECISION MAKER

Within Right-Minded Teamwork, the *Right Choice Model* uses the term "Decision-Maker" to describe the part of you that chooses to listen to and follow either the wrong-minded ways of Ego or the Right-Minded ways of Reason.

Your Decision-Maker is 100% responsible for who you choose to follow, what you choose to think, and how you choose to behave.

Right-Mindedness is achieved when you listen to and follow Reason. Listening means calming your Ego mind, trusting your intuition, and allowing space for a **moment of Reason** to arise.

When Right-Mindedness becomes an integral part of a team, the team consistently works together as one, doing no harm, within the forgiving Unified Circle of Right-Minded Thinking. When teammates do that, they are demonstrating and extending Right-Minded Teamwork to everyone.

To learn more about Reason, Ego, and the Decision-Maker, visit RightMindedTeamwork.com or your favorite book retailer and pick up the book **Reason, Ego, & the Right-Minded Teamwork Myth**: *The Philosophy & Process for Creating a Right-Minded Team That Works Together as One.* The ebook is free. It's also available in paperback.

Decision-Maker: Trust Your Intuition

If thinking about Reason and Ego are new to you, it can be helpful to think of Reason as your positive intuition and Ego as your negative, arrogant, and sometimes vindictive intuition.

At different times throughout our lives, we all have listened to and followed each of these teachers.

Stop and remember when you had a hunch or a feeling as to what you should do or say in a particular situation. Did you ignore your intuition? Let's say you did not follow your instinct, and it turned out to be a mistake. What did you say to yourself and others?

I wish I had trusted my intuition!

As this memory illustrates, **you already know how to listen and be mindful** of your intuition. It is your natural, pre-separation state of mind [See **Oneness vs. Separateness**].

You just need to do it regularly.

Decision-Making Work Agreement

Every team needs a Decision-Making Work Agreement that clearly defines how decisions are made and who makes them. Creating a general agreement and putting it into your team's Operating System's Business Plan as a team Work Agreement makes good business sense.

If you do not currently have a Decision-Making team agreement or you have not updated it recently, I highly recommend you do that as soon as it is practical.

Incidentally, Decision-Making is #18 in the *Team Performance Factor Assessment* that you will use every 90 days to keep your team focused and on track. See **Team Operating System**.

In the book, ***How to Facilitate Team Work Agreements****: A Practical, 10-Step Process for Building a Right-Minded Team That Works as One,* you will find two real agreement examples. The first one is a behavioral team Communication Work Agreement, and the other is a Decision-Making Work Agreement. Check it out and use it as a model for your team's Decision-Making Work Agreement.

Desire & Willingness:
Preconditions for Accountability

Even though the terms "desire" and "willingness" are not often mentioned in Right-Minded Teamwork materials (except within the *Right Choice Model*), Right-Mindedness and accountability are virtually synonymous.

The concepts of desire and willingness permeate all RMT methods and processes simply because it is impossible to think in a Right-Minded way, behave with Right-Minded Accountability, and achieve Right-Minded Teamwork without a heartfelt desire and genuine willingness to do so.

The *Right Choice Model* found in the book *How to Apply the Right Choice Model: Create a Right-Minded Team That Works as One* teaches, *Right-Minded Accountability is the desire and willingness to change my mind and behavior in order to effectively respond to difficult team situations.*

If you share the Right Choice Model with your team and distribute the Right Choice cards to teammates, you will see the definition of "desire and willingness" on the cards.

Ego & Ego Attack

Ego is the negative, wrong-minded teacher who continually tells you how difficult the world is and how you must constantly fight to survive.

EGO

Reason is the opposite of Ego. Reason teaches you to *do unto others as you would have them do unto you.*

Ego believes everyone is out to get you and directs you to *do unto others before they do unto you.* Ego is also the creator of the tiny, mad idea of separation presented in the *Right-Minded Teamwork Myth.*

An Ego attack is a flash of negative, out-of-control emotion. It happens when you believe the awful feeling you are experiencing has been caused by something someone else said or did to you. Without thinking, you become behaviorally triggered; your body language, tone of voice, and the words you say become mean-spirited. An Ego attack is the opposite of a **moment of Reason**.

As soon as you realize you are experiencing an Ego attack, you must train your mind to say, *I am angry. I have lost control. I'm not upset for the reason I think. I am out of my right mind. I need a moment of Reason to gain control of my attitude. I must return to the classroom so I can find a Right-Minded way of replying that allows us to do no harm and work as one.*

Interlocking Accountability

Interlocking accountability is a crucial RMT concept that is primarily used in *How to Facilitate Team Work Agreements: a Practical, 10-Step Process for Building a Right-Minded Team That Works as One.*

When your team creates Work Agreements, it is highly recommended that one of your agreements includes an interlocking accountability statement so that teammates agree, ahead of time, how to compassionately confront a teammate who continues to break your Work Agreements.

Interlocking Accountability means many things, including:

- Giving positive reinforcement when someone continues to do a great job of living the Work Agreements.
- Confronting someone in a supportive and safe but firm way if they continue to break the spirit or letter of the team's Work Agreement.
- Being accountable to each other for achieving or accomplishing the desired outcome of the Work Agreements.
- Recovering and learning from mistakes rather than denying or punishing those who make mistakes. This strengthens team spirit and trust.
- Creating and sustaining teammate trust because teammates who believe everyone will live their part of the Work Agreement will create Right-Minded Teamwork.

Moment of Reason

When you are facing a challenge such as an Ego attack, and you experience a positive and perhaps surprising moment of revelation, clarity, or sanity, you have achieved a moment of Reason.

These moments occur when you genuinely try to move from the battleground into the classroom. When Reason's teaching breaks through, you move from wrong mindedness into Right-Mindedness.

Moments of Reason are magnificent. They are a cornerstone of your Right-Minded thought system. When they happen, you feel confident and at peace. You know what you should do, what to say, and to whom.

In moments of Reason, you know beyond a shadow of a doubt that you want and need your teammates. You easily return to the Unified Circle of Right-Minded Thinking, where teammates forgive one another, do no harm, and work as one.

Onboarding New Teammates

When a new leader or teammate joins your team, it is vitally important to properly onboard them within their first week on the job. In a single short meeting where everyone attends, the onboarding is easily and effectively accomplished.

Present all your RMT goals and Work Agreements along with why they were created. They ask you clarifying questions. Afterward, you ask them to accept the team's goals and actively live the team's Work Agreements.

206 · DAN HOGAN

Oneness vs. Separateness

Oneness is a psychological state of mind. It can be described in many ways using phrases such as *None of us is as smart as all of us,* or *do no harm,* and *work as one.*

Separateness is the opposite of oneness. To become a Right-Minded teammate, you must train your mind to choose attitudes and behaviors that create and extend oneness, not project separateness.

For a list of 30 examples of oneness, see the Right-Minded Teamwork Attitudes & Behaviors list found in numerous RMT books.

The concepts and story behind oneness and separateness are introduced in RMT's book, ***Reason, Ego & the Right-Minded Teamwork Myth:*** *The Philosophy and Process for Creating a Right-Minded Team That Works Together as One.* You can pick up your ebook copy for free at RightMindedTeamwork.com or your favorite book retailer. It is also available in paperback.

In this book, you will learn about Ego's "tiny, mad idea" of wanting more "stuff" and how Ego's choices led us all into a world of separation. That tiny, mad moment was, literally, the **birth of separation**. But, as the Myth reveals, Reason is always ready to lead us back into oneness - our pre-separation state – joyfully described as the Unified Circle of Right-Minded Thinking where we can do no harm and work as one.

Preventions & Interventions

In RMT's ***Design a Right-Minded, Team-Building Workshop****: 12 Steps to Create a Team That Works as One*, the team-building facilitator and team leader meet early on to proactively identify potential issues that could keep teammates from achieving the workshop's desired outcomes.

This discussion leads to creating *preventions* that the team leader or facilitator takes to help prevent those issues from happening. The facilitator and team leader also agree on how to intervene in case the preventions don't work. Much of the time, however, preventions do their job and make *interventions* during team-building workshops unnecessary.

To learn more about effective preventions and interventions, go to RightMindedTeamwork.com or your favorite book retailer, and pick up your copy of these two books:

How to Facilitate Team Work Agreements*: A Practical, 10-Step Process for Building a Right-Minded Team That Works as One*

Design a Right-Minded, Team-Building Workshop*: 12 Steps to Create a Team That Works as One*

Psychological Goals

A team's psychological goals describe how teammates intentionally choose to think and behave as they work together to achieve their team's business goals.

Psychological goals, such as achieving mutual trust and respect among teammates, may be viewed as a team's collective school of thought, values, or thought system.

These consciously chosen goals, captured in team Work Agreements, clarify the team's principles or standards of behavior.

Here is a specific example of a psychological goal you will find in several RMT materials:

> *When difficult team situations happen, we accept, forgive, and adjust our attitudes and behavior. We always find solutions because we believe that none of us is as smart as all of us.*

Reason

Reason is a mythological character and symbolic guide who shows you how to think and behave in a Right-Minded way. As your Right-Minded teacher, Reason helps you differentiate and choose between Right-Minded and wrong-minded attitudes and behaviors.

REASON

Reason is the opposite of Ego. Whereas Ego believes everyone is out to get you and instructs you to *do unto others before they do unto you,* Reason teaches you to *do unto others as you would have them do unto you.*

Ego encourages and projects separateness.
Reason cultivates and extends oneness.

Reason is that part of your mind that always speaks for the Right Choice attitudes and behaviors. When you need a **moment of Reason** to find the best way to respond to a difficult team situation, say to yourself

I am here to be truly helpful.

I am here to represent Reason who sent me.

I do not have to worry about what to say or what to do because Reason who sent me will direct me.

When you experience a moment of Reason (a moment of revelation, clarity, or sanity regarding a particular challenge), "remembering" Reason's gentle guidance towards oneness restores your mind to the forgiving Unified Circle of Right-Minded Thinking.

For the full story of Ego's tiny, mad idea of separation and how Reason waits even today to bring us back to oneness, pick up your free copy of the ebook *Reason, Ego & the Right-Minded Teamwork Myth: The Philosophy and Process for Creating a Right-Minded Team That Works Together as One* at RightMindedTeamwork.com or your favorite book retailer. It's also available in paperback.

Reason, Ego & the Right-Minded Teamwork Myth

This book teaches two significant concepts:

- the Right-Minded Teamwork Myth, a short tale that presents RMT's underlying teamwork philosophy of doing no harm and working as one
- the Right-Minded Teamwork team-building tools, methods, and processes to create Right-Minded, productive teams.

The RMT Myth is a short, simple story. It follows three characters: Reason, Ego, and you, the Decision-Maker. Simply put, the RMT Myth and philosophy advocate for teammates to follow Reason's path of oneness instead of following Ego's disastrous advice to seek separateness and prioritize selfishness.

Following the RMT Myth, you will learn about the Right-Minded Teamwork process. Unlike the story, the RMT process is no myth. It is practical, deliberate, and reliable.

The RMT process is a set of interconnected, team-building methods that together form a self-perpetuating, continuous improvement system. This process allows you to integrate the aspirations of the RMT Myth into your team in a way that helps you achieve your business goals.

This book teaches the RMT process and provides a clear overview of the seven other RMT team-building books that, when used together, form a continuous improvement process guaranteed to support team growth and success.

Pick up your free copy at RightMindedTeamwork.com or your favorite book retailer. It is also available in paperback.

Recognition:
Make It Easy to Keep Going

Authentic recognition is not about bestowing company shirts and prizes. It is about giving and receiving genuine appreciation for a job well done.

Recognition plays a critical role in growing your team's business because it keeps your team's spirit ignited. Unfortunately, many people work in team environments where there is little to no recognition. These teammates are discouraged. They do not give their best to the team. Why should they?

Discouraged teammates are like racehorses. If a horse is giving you only 80%, you can whip him, and he will give you 90%. Whip him again, and he will give you 100%. But if you whip him again, after he has already given you everything he has, he will drop back to 80%, or maybe even less. He has learned that you are going to whip him regardless, even if he works harder. So why should he give you his best?

Whipped people leave teams.

Far too often, the ones who leave are the most talented teammates. People that receive legitimate and genuine recognition stay and contribute. Shirts and prizes cannot earn that kind of loyalty or effort.

In the book *Right-Minded Teamwork: 9 Right Choices for Building a Team That Works as One*, you will learn that Recognition is one of the 9 Right Choices.

See **Critical Few: Complete Important Tasks First**. for a related concept.

Right Choice Model

The *Right Choice Model* is an effective teaching aid that will help you and your teammates choose your own set of unique, "right" teamwork attitudes and behaviors.

Inspired by *A Course in Miracles*, *The Right Choice Model* consists of two circles. The upper loop of acceptance, forgiveness, and adjustment represents the Unified Circle of Right-Minded Thinking.

The lower loop of rejection, Ego attack, and defensiveness describes the separated or divided circle of wrong-minded thinking.

To learn more about this simple but powerful teaching model, go to RightMindedTeamwork.com or your favorite book retailer, and pick up your copy of *How to Apply the Right Choice Model: Create a Right-Minded Team That Works as One*.

Right-Minded Teamwork's 5 Element Framework

Right-Minded Teamwork is a business-oriented, psychological approach to team building where acceptance, forgiveness, and adjustment are teammate characteristics, and 100% customer satisfaction is the team's result.

Right-Minded Teamwork is built off a framework of 5 Elements consisting of two goals and three teamwork methods.

1. Team **Business Goal**: Achieve 100% Customer Satisfaction
2. Team **Psychological Goal**: Commit to Right-Minded Thinking
3. Team **Work Agreements**: Create & Follow Commitments
4. **Team Operating System**: Make It Effective & Efficient
5. **Right-Minded Teammates**: Strengthen Individual Performance

To learn more, go to RightMindedTeamwork.com or your favorite book retailer, and pick up your copy of ***Right-Minded Teamwork in Any Team***: *The Ultimate Team-Building Method to Create a Team That Works as One.*

Right-Minded Teamwork's 5 Element Implementation Plan

There is no one right way to implement RMT's 5 Element but the three-workshop plan presented in the book *Right-Minded Teamwork in Any Team: The Ultimate Team-Building Method to Create a Team That Works as One* has proven effective countless times.

Here's a brief overview.

First Workshop
Create **psychological goals** plus at least one **Work Agreement**.

Second Workshop
Reaffirm **business goals** and agree on a **Team Operating System**.

Third Workshop
Encourage and support Right-Minded **Teammate development**.

After the third workshop, and every 90 days after that, you will apply RMT's *Team Operating System & Performance Factor Assessment* to identify opportunities, take action, and achieve new teamwork improvements.

Right-Minded Teamwork
Attitudes & Behaviors

The Right-Minded Teamwork model includes a list of 30 behavioral and process-oriented teammate attitudes and behaviors with their associated costs and benefits. I collected and compiled these over three decades of team-building workshops.

This valuable list includes clear, specific, right, and wrong behaviors "taught" to us by either Reason or Ego.

Thoughts and attitudes always precede teamwork behavior. Right-Minded attitudes come from Reason. Wrong-minded attitudes come from Ego.

The good news is that Right-Minded attitudes are natural. They are already inside you and your teammates. When you think about any of the wrong-minded Ego attitudes listed you will see in the list, ask yourself,

> *Was I born with these depressing, debilitating, and awful attitudes?*

Your answer will always be **"no!"** You learned those wrong-minded attitudes from Ego. That means *you can unlearn them, too.*

You can find the list in several RMT books, including ***How to Apply the Right Choice Model****: Create a Right-Minded Team That Works as One*, available at RightMindedTeamwork.com or your favorite book retailer.

Right-Mindedness vs. Wrong-Mindedness

"Mindedness" is what you choose to think and perceive. Right-Mindedness refers to the positive mental state, perceptions, choices, and actions you demonstrate when following Reason's guidance.

Wrong mindedness refers to the negative mental state that occurs when you follow Ego's advice.

> *Mindfulness is a journey without distance to a goal **you want to achieve**.*

In the book ***How to Apply the Right Choice Model****: Create a Right-Minded Team That Works as One*, you will find a list of rewards and consequences for choosing Right-Mindedness.

In the book *7 **Mindfulness Training Lessons***: *Improve Teammates' Ability to Work as One with Right-Minded Thinking*, you will learn that in every circumstance, and especially during difficult team situations, Right-Minded Teammates practice mindfulness, or Right-Mindedness, to move them into an ally-focused way of thinking and behaving.

Both of these books will help you accept that your mind is split between two thought systems. At one moment, you are following Reason, and the next, Ego. It is impossible to create and sustain Right-Minded Thinking with a split mind. To heal your split mind, you want to apply the *7 Mindful Training Lessons* and the *Right Choice Model's* attitudes and behaviors.

To bring your team back into the forgiving Unified Circle of Right-Minded Thinking, pick up your copy of these books at your favorite book retailer or RightMindedTeamwork.com.

RMT Motto: Do No Harm. Work as One.

The Right-Minded philosophy is founded on two universal truths:

None of us is as smart as all of us.
Right-Minded Teammates know that working collaboratively together, in a Right-Minded manner, is the only way to create the kind of teamwork that achieves and sustains 100% customer satisfaction. Said differently, these teammates genuinely want and need their fellow teammates.

Do no harm and work as one.
As a Right-Minded Teammate, you can be firm, direct, gentle, and compassionate, all at the same time. You do not blame yourself or others for mistakes. You and your teammates are allies, not adversaries, working together towards your shared goals.

RMT Facilitator

The RMT Facilitator has a special function. Simply put, their expert facilitation *transforms* well-meaning dysfunctional souls into *healthy and functional teammates*.

Using the array of RMT tools, the RMT Facilitator guides teammates in converting their team mistakes into *do-no-harm-work-as-one* attitudes and behaviors.

Teammates are perpetually grateful for the RMT facilitator's help in achieving and sustaining Right-Minded Teamwork. Some even say their RMT Facilitator *saved them*. Team leaders and teammates continually seek the RMT Facilitator's support for years to come.

Team transformations are the RMT Facilitator's **special function**.

218 · DAN HOGAN

Team Management System:
An RMT Enterprise-Wide Process

An enterprise's Team Management System (TMS) aligns all teammate attitudes and work behavior throughout the organization. An effective TMS ensures everyone is doing their part to help the organization achieve the enterprise's vision, mission, and strategic goals.

RMT's Team Management System involves integrating RMT's 5-Element Framework into all teams.

1. Team **Business Goal**: Achieve 100% Customer Satisfaction
2. Team **Psychological Goal**: Commit to Right-Minded Thinking
3. Team **Work Agreements**: Create & Follow Commitments
4. **Team Operating System**: Make It Effective & Efficient
5. **Right-Minded Teammates**: Strengthen Individual Performance

To learn more, go to RightMindedTeamwork.com or your favorite book retailer, and purchase your copy of ***Achieve Your Organization's Strategic Plan***: *Create a Right-Minded, Team Management System to Ensure All Teams Work as One.*

Team Operating System &
Performance Factor Assessment

RMT's Team Operating System is a six-step, 90-day, continuous improvement operating system that organizes your team functions to increase the likelihood of achieving customer satisfaction.

The system also includes the *Team Performance Factor Assessment* [step 3], which you will use to help teammates identify two to three improvement opportunities every 90 days.

The 25 performance factors in this assessment are aligned with and thus measure the six steps of RMT's Team Operating System. They effectively measure all aspects of Right-Minded Teamwork.

If you want your team to operate more effectively and efficiently, apply this 90-day process after your team has completed the first three RMT workshops. For a brief explanation, see in this glossary: *Right-Minded Teamwork's 5 Element Implementation Plan*.

Apply the three-workshop plan and the operating system, and you nearly guarantee your team will create Right-Minded Teamwork.

To learn the process, go to RightMindedTeamwork.com or your favorite book retailer, and pick up your copy of **Right-Minded Teamwork in Any Team:** *The Ultimate Team-Building Method to Create a Team That Works as One.*

Thought System

What you believe *is* your thought system. Pause and reflect on this truth, and above all, be thankful that it is true.

Whether you are consciously aware of it or not, your thought system is the lens through which you view the world. Without exception, everyone has one. And though there are many variations, there are *only two thought systems* from which to choose:

- A Right-Minded thought system, which extends ally beliefs of acceptance, forgiveness, and adjustment to everyone, everywhere, forever
- A wrong-minded system, which projects adversarial assaults of rejection, attack, and defensiveness to everyone, everywhere, forever

Once you have developed a thought system of any kind, you live it and teach it. Even if you are not entirely aware of it, it remains at the forefront of your mind, influencing your daily behaviors and choices.

If your thought system is negative, or you choose to follow Ego into an unnecessary and adversarial competition, you cannot be a happy, successful teammate.

To live in the land of oneness where your workplace is a safe and supportive classroom and where you and your teammates work as one to achieve team goals, you must train your mind and align your thought system with the teachings of Reason.

There is no possible compromise between these two thought systems. You either collaborate, or you compete. When you follow Ego, you take your team to the battleground. When you choose to follow Reason, you willingly create and genuinely strive to live your team's Work Agreements. With Reason's help, you transform your team into a lovely, collaborative, successful classroom.

The choice is clear.

Reject Ego. Embrace Reason.

Be Thankful.

Train Your Mind

When your mind is well-trained in Reason's Decision-Making ways, Ego attacks do not throw you off course. When a difficult team situation happens, you immediately stop for a **moment of Reason**. You refocus on oneness, rise above the battleground, and remember to live your Work Agreements in your classroom.

To train your mind simply means practicing your team's Work Agreements, which represent your psychological goals, as often as possible, especially during difficult team situations.

Uncovering Root Cause

The Right-Minded Teamwork philosophy advocates leaders, teammates, and facilitators resolve the root cause of teamwork issues instead of making the mistake of addressing symptoms.

Though this view is discussed in many RMT materials, uncovering the root cause is heavily emphasized as a core concept in the book *Design a Right-Minded, Team-Building Workshop: 12 Steps to Create a Team That Works as One.*

Inside that book, you will find a story about a well-meaning team leader who asked me, as their team-building facilitator, if I could teach a three-day workshop in just two days. He believed a quick team event would address the problem he saw in his team.

But the problem he was seeing was only the symptom, not the root cause of the issue. Had I agreed and given him what he asked for, the team would still be struggling with the same issue. And, as a facilitator, I would have failed both the team and the leader.

Instead, by pausing to look for the root cause of the team challenge first, we ended up designing and executing a practical, Right-Minded Teamwork workshop to solve the actual underlying problem.

By seeking out the root cause first, we delivered the leader's desired result, even though the workshop we held was not what he had initially asked for.

To improve your ability to uncover root causes and read this short story, go to your favorite book retailer or RightMindedTeamwork.com and pick up your copy of *Design a Right-Minded, Team-Building Workshop: 12 Steps to Create a Team That Works as One.*

Unified Circle of Right-Minded Thinking

When your team discusses and agrees on your psychological goals – your consciously chosen set of attitudes and behaviors as described in your Work Agreements – you have created your team's collective thought system.

By uniting with each other in this way and openly committing to one another through your Work Agreements, you are renouncing Ego in yourself and your teammates and collectively committing to train your minds to follow Reason.

This process of creating team Work Agreements is your undivided declaration of interdependence. Your assertion is saying,

> *We hold these mindful truths to be self-evident that all minds are created equal, and whosoever believes that will have everlasting freedom to choose Right-Minded Teamwork.*

Your declaration plus your daily acts of living your team Work Agreements *is your return* to the forgiving Unified Circle Right-Minded Thinking.

Work Agreements

A Work Agreement is a collective promise made by teammates to transform non-productive, adversarial behavior into collaborative teamwork behavior. Work Agreements are a key tool for teammates and teams who aspire to do no harm and work as one.

Work Agreements are not flimsy ground rules. They are emotionally mature work performance commitments. Work Agreements announce your dedication to oneness and demonstrate your inner belief that *none of us is as smart as all of us.*

Your team's collective Work Agreements also define your team's psychological goals and thought system. They ensure you conduct your day-to-day work from within your team's Unified Circle of Right-Minded Thinking.

To learn more about the power of Work Agreements and how to use them to transform your team, go to RightMindedTeamwork.com or your favorite book retailer, and pick up your copy of ***How to Facilitate Team Work Agreements****: A Practical, 10-Step Process for Building a Right-Minded Team That Works as One.*

Resources

Reusable Resources

& Templates

for

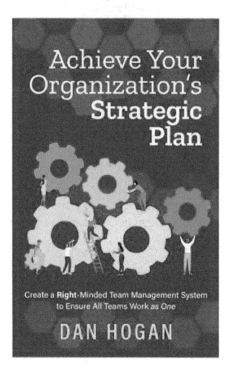

Achieve Your
Organization's
Strategic
Plan

Create a **Right**-Minded Team Management System
to Ensure All Teams Work as *One*

DAN HOGAN

Reusable Resources & Templates

You already have these *Reusable Resources & Templates* if you purchased this book package at RightMindedTeamwork.com.

But if you purchased this book elsewhere, you may also have the *Reusable Resources & Templates* for a special discounted price.

Go to RightMindedTeamwork.com and search for *Reusable Resources & Templates for Achieve Your Organization's Strategic Plan* to obtain these valuable resources.

These materials are only available at RightMindedTeamwork.com.

When you purchase these *Reusable Resources & Templates*, you will be downloading PDF and Microsoft Word files that contain these reusable materials:

- ✓ Steering Team Charter & 90-Day Implementation Plan
- ✓ An Orientation: Introducing Our Team Management System
- ✓ Five Reusable Agenda Templates
- ✓ Right-Minded Teamwork Attitudes & Behaviors
- ✓ RMT's Team Performance Factor Assessment
- ✓ RMT Infographic Models

To Buy These Reusable Resources & Templates

1. Go to RightMindedTeamwork.com

2. Click to the Reusable Resources tab

3. Search for **Reusable Resources & Templates** for ***Achieve Your Organization's Strategic Plan:*** *Create a Right-Minded Team Management System to Ensure All Teams Work Together as One*

4. Add to Cart to Download

Use discount code **TMS** for 15% off regular price

RMT Implementation Plan – 4 Actual Examples

Four Actual RMT Implementation Plans: Results

Example #1 Nuclear Power Generating Plant

Results: The senior leadership team created and deployed a 100-Day Behavioral Outage that transformed the employee culture. Using RMT's Work Agreement process and other tools, this courageous **improvement project** succeeded and was featured in *Nuclear News*.

Example #2 Field Support Team

Results: This self-managing team, in one year, increased its teammate trust by 78% and saved their organization $350,000 when they successfully used RMT's **behavioral Work Agreement** process and the Three Workshop Implementation Plan.

Example #3 International Project Team

Results: This major capital project team immediately saved $10,000 a week in labor costs when they successfully used RMT's **process Work Agreement** to streamline their meetings.

Example #4 Architectural Design Company

Results: This firm had a good problem. Their business revenue had increased 100% in the past twelve months. They grew from 50 to 100 employees practically overnight, and they were still growing. They needed a strategic plan and operating structure. Using **RMT's Three Workshop Implementation Plan** plus team **Work Agreements**, they succeeded.

Four Actual RMT Implementation Plans: Overview

Example #1

The first example describes my work with a nuclear power generating plant with 500 employees. They used many RMT processes, including team Work Agreements and the Right Choice Model.

This example is presented a little differently than the other three. After you read a short synopsis, you will read an industry article from Nuclear News that described the seven behavioral modifications that compromised what they named their **100-Day Behavior Outage.**

Examples #2 - #4

In the last three examples, I will show you how these teams used RMT's three-workshop Implementation Plan to achieve team improvement. Specifically, you will see what they accomplished in their first, second, and third workshops.

For each team, you will find a short description of what the team did as well as their actual Team Business Plan.

You don't need to conduct a detailed review of each plan.

Instead, use these plans as templates. These examples will give you positive ideas about creating your own Right-Minded Teamwork Implementation Plan and your Team Business Plan.

Example #1: Nuclear Power Generating Plant
Prairie Island's 100-day Behavior Outage

Synopsis

Facing a potential shutdown from their credentialing agency after a significant performance decline, Joel Sorensen, Vice President of the Prairie Island Nuclear Power Plant, knew things needed to change. So, he implemented Right-Minded Teamwork's Work Agreements and Right Choice "Accountability Model to support the plant-wide culture change plan.

Be sure to read Joel's comments in second modification about accountability and work agreements.

"If you had asked me two months ago if the leadership team would reach this level of performance, my answer would have been emphatically, "NO!" Now that we are on this road, I don't ever want to go back." ~ Joel Sorensen

Joel gave this interview to the Nuclear News that tells the story.

THE NUCLEAR NEWS INTERVIEW

Prairie Island's 100-day Behavior Outage
Changing employees' culture requires a site-wide plan and site-wide participation.

A100-day outage at Prairie Island didn't shut down power production, but it did change the way the plant operates. Called a "Behavior Outage," the program was aimed at altering employee culture at Prairie Island. The outage ran from last August to November and was modeled after refueling and maintenance outages in having specific plans and goals.

The Behavior Outage has helped reduce human performance errors at Prairie Island. Outage plans called on employees to examine their attitudes while changing behaviors that contributed to unpredictable performance. *Joel Sorensen*, Prairie Island's site vice president, and his management team developed the concept for the Behavior Outage. They initiated it by first calling for an assessment of plant operations to highlight those areas where improvements were most needed. These included change management communications, accountability, leadership, human performance work practices, corrective action, work management, and outage preparation.

The two-unit Prairie Island plant, in Red Wing, Minn., is operated by Nuclear Management Company (NMC). The two units are Westinghouse pressurized water reactors, each rated at 535-MWe (net). The interview was conducted by Rick Michal, NN senior associate editor.

Could you explain the history of the Behavior Outage at Prairie Island?

I solicited some retired nuclear executives to help me understand where our organization was going, whether it was improving or not. Those executives came to Prairie Island the first week of August 2000 and did a self-assessment. As a result, a report they prepared showed that while plant performance had improved over the short term, our organizational effectiveness had been flat for a long time and was remaining flat. We used that report to spur our organization to break out of past behaviors and start moving ahead. The assessment showed that in order for us to have good long-term plant performance, we needed to have good behaviors on the part of our workers, managers, and supervisors.

How did you come up with 100 days for the outage?

We felt we needed to put some urgency on this. We didn't want another plan that would take months and months to execute and where we wouldn't see results. So, we decided to put together a plan to work on behaviors and get results within 100 days. Once we decided on a plan that had a sense of urgency, we decided to treat it like we would a plant refueling outage. For the Behavior Outage, there would be specific outage plans, outage schedules, and daily outage meetings to follow our progress. We patterned it after a refueling outage because we needed a similar way of doing business to get the results we wanted for our behaviors. We felt we could keep both units running safely while spending 100 days focusing on our behaviors.

What did it cost Prairie Island to conduct this outage, and did you bring in an outside vendor to help conduct it?

It doesn't cost much money to work on behaviors. We formed employee cross-disciplinary teams to help develop plans for each of seven focus areas we identified that needed improvement. These seven areas we called "behavior modifications." But we needed help because we were struggling with accountability as a behavior. So, we partnered with a private firm—**Lord & Hogan LLC, based in Houston, Texas [creator of Right-Minded Teamwork]**—to help us understand what accountability means and to work with us on accountable behaviors.

Could you talk specifically about your seven behavior modifications?

Most emphasis for behavior modification was put on our management team as leaders of the plant, but every part of the organization, from supervisors to workers, was engaged in this activity. I'll explain each modification individually:

Our first modification is change management communications, because we lacked a consistent way of implementing change. We put in place a change management model, which contains a step-by-step process, and we use it to implement all other changes we need to make. We also realized that communication had to be effective in order to instill these behavior changes across the organization, so we focused on improving internal communications between plant departments. The plan includes a mix of print, electronic, and face-to-face methods—with a strong emphasis on increased frequency of communications and greater supervisor communication with employees.

The second modification is accountability. During the 100 days, we worked on developing accountability agreements [now called **team Work Agreements**], which laid out how our managers should treat each other with regard to trust and respect. We also empowered a cross section of employees to go out and train their peers on the meaning of accountability. There is no financial incentive for living up to the accountability agreement, but what we find is that when we live these agreements, work becomes much more rewarding. We continue to adopt accountability agreements throughout the rest of the organization.

The **third modification** is leadership, and assessments were done for our entire leadership team. Every station manager received an assessment of his or her strengths and weaknesses. Each manager then developed a personal development plan, and they are now living and working that plan.

The **fourth modification** is human performance work practices. We put together two teams, one being a cross-section of workers and the other a cross-section of supervisors, that developed a common set of tools for use by plant employees to prevent human error events. These tools are self-checking, procedure use and adherence, communication standards, peer-checking, and "tail-gating" sessions.

Each **week during** the Behavior Outage we focused on one of these tools to help us understand how to use it in preventing human errors. For example, the "tail-gating" session is something we want all of our employees to work through before they start any task. We want them to be able to summarize the task, anticipate what might go wrong, foresee any consequences, and evaluate what tools could be used to prevent errors. It's a mental checklist for them to use and to discuss with their co-workers before they go out on any task.

Peer checking, of all of the tools, is the one I'm most impressed with regarding how the team came up with it. Peer-checking is common in the industry, but the twist our folks put on it is by actively caring. Generally, people in Minnesota are viewed as near the top in the nation in caring. To carry this active caring to the nuclear plant was innovative and something we continue to build on.

Our behaviors prior to the 100-day outage were "conflict avoidant," which meant that people would avoid conflict. But that has changed. I'll give you an example. A general laborer here recently confronted an operator who was standing above the top safety step on a ladder. This entry-level laborer said to the veteran operator, "Hey, you're not following the ladder safety practices. Why don't you let me help you down and I will help you find a ladder that is the right height for this job." Prior to this, it would have been easy for the laborer to walk by and not confront the operator on the ladder. But when that operator got down from the ladder, he turned to the laborer and said, "Thank you."

The **fifth modification** is corrective action, which plays off putting our accountability behaviors into practice. As an entire organization, we were allowing our corrective action backlog to become overdue, knowing it would grow. But strictly by using highly accountable behavior, we were able to complete 1410 corrective actions and 917 procedure changes in our backlog. We reduced our overdue items from about 300 corrective actions that were overdue to zero. These were all completed during the 100-day Behavior Outage. This was done strictly by holding people accountable, and by completing things when we said we would complete them.

The **sixth modification** is work management. Our human performance staff told us that if we didn't fix our work management process, we'd never be able to eliminate human performance events or equipment performance events. Our existing process had been burdensome and ineffective, so we put together a team to overhaul work management. That team learned we didn't have to start from scratch. There were already some good standard processes laid out here and we just needed to work on implementing them. The team put together an implementation plan within the 100 days by using our change management plan process. We are working now to implement the team's plan completely.

The **seventh modification** is outage preparation. In the past, we would allow outage milestones to come and go and not be met. But through accountability, we were, for example, able to make sure we met our pre-outage milestones in preparing for Unit 1's refueling outage last January. For that outage, we achieved approximately a 21 percent reduction in overall outage length compared to our refueling over the previous 10 years encompassing 11 refueling outages. Much of that reduction was due to the preoutage preparation. I also credit it to the accountability behaviors on the part of our staff that executed the refueling outage—getting people to own issues, take actions, and commit to completion dates. I saw good results during the outage in the area of emergent issues that came up. Because of these accountable behaviors, we were able to identify, own, and correct emergent issues so they didn't become threats to the outage schedule.

How did the employees react when they were told there was going to be a Behavior Outage?

We had to create dissatisfaction with the status quo. I wanted everyone dissatisfied with the current state of affairs, the state of our organizational ineffectiveness. What we did was gather all the employees together for a "fire and brimstone" meeting to let them know we were not satisfied with the way things were working at Prairie Island. We all needed to change, including me.

We then laid out the plan and a new vision for the facility that focused on the long term. We had to get people thinking about what we needed to do to be an industry leader. We then set the plan in place, worked the plan, and at the end of the outage we celebrated the accomplishments.

As you went deeper into the Behavior Outage, did you see the culture changing among employees?

We, as an organization, started reading everything we could on changing culture. We recognized that our organization followed what the textbooks said about change: Roughly 20 percent of the organization jumps on board immediately and is helpful as change agents, about 50 percent of the organization sits on the fence waiting to see if it's "real" or not, and 30 percent resists change. We were aware we would need to face these resistors, but we didn't spend a lot of time on them. We focused instead on championing the change agents to help us drive the new culture.

With the Behavior Outage over, has the work force embraced the culture change?

What you're asking about is momentum. As a management team we recognize when we're letting the momentum slip, and I'm extremely pleased with our ability to recognize that. The management team owns that and jumps on it right away to make adjustments to keep the energy level up and the changes going. Can I say that we have driven to 100 percent on our change agents? No, but we continue to work hard at driving the highly accountable behaviors throughout all of our supervisors and entire work force.

Do you know if any other nuclear plants in the U.S. or internationally have conducted an outage like this?

Not to my knowledge. Certainly, organizations recognize that in order to get good results they need to have good behaviors. But it's difficult to drive those behavior changes throughout an organization.

Did any department at Prairie Island benefit more than others because of the Behavior Outage?

One of the things we're striving for is to break down "department silos" [isolation]. The fact that our managers think first as station managers and then as department managers puts a contrary spin on that question. I'd say the site benefited most by knocking the silos down between departments.

Is this type of outage going to be conducted at other NMC nuclear plants?

It's a matter of timing at each individual site. But the NMC is looking hard at modeling our accountability because we do want to work on accountability across our fleet of plants.

Has Prairie Island become a trendsetter by having a Behavior Outage?

When we return to being an industry leader, I will answer your question.

Example #2: Field Support Team

Synopsis

A Field Operations team for an international oil and gas production company operating in the Gulf of Mexico called and asked me to help them. They were responsible for supporting all the company's offshore oil platforms.

Though team members were competent, they weren't happy. And they were far from productive. Worst of all, two-thirds of the team members were arrogant and overly aggressive.

After identifying team business goals and psychological goals, I guided them toward creating two Work Agreements: a behavioral Agreement to improve trust and a process Agreement to become a self-managing team.

Just one year later, the team had completely turned around.

They had recommitted to their shared goals and were honoring their Work Agreements. As a result, they experienced:

- 78% increase in teammate trust
- 46% increase in mutual team member support
- 61% increase in complying with decisions
- Over $350,000 in savings

For a **more detailed description** of this team's first year with RMT, go to RightMindedTeamwrok.com, search for and read *How to Create Team Working Agreements That Bring People Together*.

First Workshop

I worked with this team for two years. We met every three months for a total of eight workshops. The first workshop was a two-day event; the others were one-day events.

In the first workshop, we created two Agreements.

The team's "relationships Agreement" addressed such things as proper communication, how to behave when a conflict occurs, and a commitment to resolve any unresolved teamwork issues.

The second Agreement addressed team meetings. Since the team had been recently instructed to become self-managing, conducting efficient and effective meetings was a top priority.

Second & Third Workshops

In the next two workshops, the team created a peer-to-peer assessment process. They also made team strategies that aligned with their profit center's strategic goals.

Below are their actual Team Business Plan and Work Agreements. The plan presented here was their second plan, created at the end of their first year.

Additionally, you'll see the results of their Team Performance Assessment Summary, which shows one full year of improvement data.

Large International Oil & Gas Company

Field Support Team's
- Safety & Tactical Plan
- Our Team Business Plan

Who We Are & What We Value

Our goal is to become a high-performing, self-managing team. This Team Business Plan includes the most updated perspectives and strategies for our team.

Who is the "Team?"
Mike: Facilities Representative
Will: Facilities Representative
Mark: Facilities Representative
Sam: Facilities Representative
Bob: Measurement Specialist
Steve: Workover Representative
Steve: Paint / Corrosion Representative

Our Commitment:

As a member of this team, I attest to being an active participant in creating this Team Business Plan and these Work Agreements.

I commit to hold myself accountable and to adhere to them to the best of my ability.

Field Support Team's Business Safety Plan
"Committed to Excellence in Safety"

1. **Full Implementation of STOP Program**
   A. STOP program to be used on ALL projects supervised. Encourage participation by contractor and operations personnel.
      a. Route all STOP cards through the MPS who will compile data and forward to E&S Champions for wide distribution of STOP recap report. Track contractor and company participation separately.
      b. MPS to use the graphical presentation of data for posting as per E&S format.
   B. Track "Near Misses" through the use of the STOP program.
      a. E&S Champions to track "Near Misses" on a separate recap report for use at weekly FSG meetings.

2. **Safety Meetings / Information-Sharing**
   A. Discuss safety issues during weekly FST morning meetings.
      o Standing agenda items.
         ▪ Review PDN policies or regulatory updates
         ▪ Review previous hitch safety-related issues
         ▪ Review Safety Alerts
      o Discuss working contractors' recent safety performance & practices to identify potential problems.
      o List action items.

B. Hold a pre-job meeting with contractor Supervisors and Safety Reps.

- Perform pre-job walk-through on-location with contract Superintendents, Safety Reps and Company Reps
- Perform hazards / safety risks assessment.
- Require ALL contractors to submit JSA before starting work in the field.
- Review the scope of work and safety guidelines.
- Hold a post-job meeting with key personnel and share Plus / Delta's with the group.

C. Daily "Operational" Offshore Safety Meeting

- Conduct meetings in cooperation with the contractor's Foreman / Supervisor / Safety Reps.
- Identify high potential hazards associated with day's planned activities.
  - o Use JSA as a working document for daily safety meetings.
- Review previous day's Stop Cards.
- Include safety meeting topics and discussion in daily construction reports.
- Maintain a list of attendees. Keep a list in the job file.
- Perform Level 4 reviews as Standard Operating Procedure. Encourage operations participation.
- g. Conduct tailgate discussions throughout the day as the scope of work progresses to enhance safety awareness.
- Document on FST daily safety meeting forms.

D. Utilize E&S Champions.
- Work closely with E&S to review / critique / develop effective safety meeting agendas.
- Include E&S Champions in field trips to review job scope with contractors to help in identifying potential safety hazards.
- Include E&S Champions in ALL accident Root Cause Analysis.
- Include E&S Champions when possible, to assist in performing top side surveys to identify safety / compliance-related issues for maintenance work.

3. **Our Team Commitment**
   A. Full support of Team Interaction Agreements for Safety
   - Continue to participate in all team safety training & development workshops.
   - Increase focus on team success in safety.
   - Celebrate our accomplishments and acknowledge our opportunities to improve safety performance as a group.
   - Recognize our diverse workgroup. The team will support individual efforts in safety training and development for the good of the team.

   B. Provide effective communication of safety issues through Team Peer-to-Peer Process.
   - 100% team support of peer-to-peer efforts of honest, open, ongoing communication & feedback to accomplish our safety plan.

4. **Contractor Safety**
   A. Recognize outstanding contractor safety efforts and participation as appropriate.

Team Direction & Strategies

The four strategies listed below are the profit center's strategies. Included are our team's tactics and goals for addressing each strategy.

SS/EI Field Support Strategic Alignment Tactical Plan

Strategy 1 - Aggressively pursue implementation of PP&E

Champions & Responsibilities:
Will & Mark, they will:
- Collect and review all pertinent data every month to make sure the team is on track to accomplish yearly goals.
- Report back to the team.

Tactic 1: Continue to assess risk associated with construction projects through continued implementation of the FST Safety Plan.

Tactic 2: All members are trained in Root Cause Analysis. Perform RCA on near misses, ALL recordable accidents, and spills on construction and maintenance projects. Focus on information-sharing with peers and contractors.

Tactic 3: Continued support of the Contractor Safety Summary / Vendor Retention as a tool in contractor selection. Focus on feedback to E&S and Alliance sponsors on contractor performance.

Tactic 4: Continued use of Self-Review Process performing Level 4 surveys on all construction / maintenance / paint projects. Communicate efforts and results to operations and Facilities Engineers.

Tactic 5: Continue to require 100% reporting of accidents and environmental incidents.

Metrics:
1. Contractor Accident Incident Rate. Goal = IR 3.86
2. # Of Environmental Incidents due to construction. Goal = 2
3. # Of Level 4 Self Reviews performed. Goal = # of AFE projects supervised or greater
4. # Of RCA performed on incidents. Goal = 100% of recordables

Team Agreements
1. Each team member commits to accurate and timely reporting of contractor man-hours; all accidents, types, and number; environmental incidents; level 4 reviews; and all RCA's.

Strategy 2 - Proactively manage our portfolio.

Champions & Responsibilities:
Mike / Steve, they will:
- Track information and report back to the team.
- When the team is not meeting its metrics, the team commits to discuss and agree on how it can get back on track.

Tactic 1: Use surplus equipment and materials as available, utilizing procurement systems in place for determining availability.

Tactic 2: Work closely with FEs to develop AFE project objectives, cost estimates, and tracking processes to effectively meet goals. Examples: pre-job planning, daily cost reporting

Tactic 3: Active support and participation with FMTs in the MOC process.

Tactic 4: Work with Alliance Partners (suppliers) to achieve an inventory of needed stock for delivery in support of AFIS and vendor reduction efforts.

Metrics

1. Shut-in Time (actual vs estimated). Goal = +/- 15% (adjusted for changes in scope of work)
2. AFE costs (actual vs estimated). Goal = +/- 10% (adjusted for changes in scope of work)
3. $ saved by utilization of surplus equipment and materials. Goal = $100M

Team Agreements

1. Each team member will supply champions with needed data, i.e., enough information to justify adjustments for changes in the scope of work.
2. We gladly accept being held accountable for AFEs and downtime we help to plan.

Strategy 3 - Employ Total Quality Management (TQM) to manage our business.

Champions & Responsibilities:
Sam / Bob, they will:

*   Announce dates for Alignment sessions and AFIS training.
*   Track FST "paid-on-time" invoice statistics.
*   Catalog FST Work Process Improvement documentation.

Tactic 1: Identify and prioritize key work processes by discipline, as necessary.

Tactic 2: Flowchart, measure, and improve key work processes that add the highest value to the team (80 / 20).

Tactic 3: Network with Field Support in WCPC to improve info-sharing of best practices and lessons learned.

Tactic 4: Active participation in updates of FST efforts and results at the Strategic Alignment Sessions.

Tactic 5: Support of Alliance Partners with a strong focus on feedback to sponsors in identifying opportunities for improvement.

Tactic 6: Continued consideration of small, disabled, and women-owned / minority businesses in the vendor selection process.

Tactic 7: Support of AFIS accounting system implementation and vendor reduction effort.

Metrics
1. Updates on efforts at Strategic Alignment Sessions. Goal = 3
2. Team participation in AFIS training and usage. Goal = 100%
3. % Of paid-on-time invoices. Goal = 88%
4. # Of key work processes measured and improved. Goal = 2 a year
5. # Of best practices workshops with WCPC field support reps. Goal = semi-annually

Team Agreements
1. Each person will give any work process improvements to champions.
2. Team members will provide evidence of support of the alliance partners and the use of small, disabled, or minority businesses through feedback documentation.

Strategy 4 - Build a committed team and become the "work location of choice."

Champions & Responsibilities:
Mark / Steve, they will:

- Track FST progress toward achieving our metrics and report back to the team.

Tactic 1: Continue informal PMP process as a coaching tool for individual and team performance. Conduct formal individual performance reviews / self-assessments, as necessary.

Tactic 2: Continue to develop and refine the "peer-to-peer" feedback process between team members.

Tactic 3: Continue to practice and refine customer / supplier feedback processes through effective post-job reviews. Focus on improved info-sharing of lessons learned.

Tactic 4: Participate in weekly crew change communication meetings and monthly FE meetings as needed.

Tactic 5: Continue formal team training sessions to improve team interaction and develop new skills.

Tactic 6: 100% commitment and participation by team members in FSG G&A cost-reduction effort. Full support of PC and BU initiatives and info-sharing with peers and O&M to understand and support business drivers guiding cost-reduction efforts.

Tactic 7: Develop consistent guidelines for contractor and company R&A / safety performance recognition to monitor and control costs.

Metrics

1. Team Interaction Questionnaire scores. Goal = 3 times a year
2. # Of post job reviews. Goal = 100% of construction / paint AFEs.
3. Formal Peer-to-Peer team communication exercises. Goal = semi-annually
4. 55% reduction in personal T&E.
5. Monitor cost associated with contractor & company R&A / safety performance recognition awards initiated by FST.
6. Review Team Business Plan semi-annually.

Team Agreements

1. Each team member commits to do their part in completing the above metrics.

Team Performance Factors

As a team, we agreed to evaluate ourselves every quarter and to use these performance factors to keep us on track.

Here are our subjective evaluation criteria:

√ + = we are doing very well
√ = we are doing okay or average
√ - = we need to improve; we're below average
- = we are not doing this, or we are not doing this very well

Performance Factors [one of their assessments]

1. We are a dynamic team constantly measuring our performance and contributions to the profit center. √
2. We function and interact at such a high level that adjusting our efforts as business needs dictate is an integral part of our process.√

3. As a team, we communicate and function as a "family" on all issues, knowing and trusting that we all have each other's interests in mind. √

4. We recognize and appreciate (value) our differences and similarities and honor our right to be individuals. √

5. We understand, as individuals with our personal preferences and feelings, that personal sacrifice for the good of the team will be a necessary part of our work at certain times. √

6. Our team interaction is at such a high level that sharing responsibility and accountability is never an issue. √−

7. Our personal and professional relationships among team members make recognition and celebration of each other's efforts a naturally occurring part of our team process. −

8. We are a leader in the safety and environmental arena because we adhere to our Field Support Team Safety Plan. √+

9. We have a team culture that is open, honest, and fun. √

10. We optimize available resources for our portfolio management by utilizing surplus equipment, sharing manpower, sharing expertise, etc. √+

11. We meet with customers regularly to discuss expectations, form partnerships, and gain feedback on performance. −

12. Each member knows and accepts their role and responsibilities as they pertain to the team. √

13. We take intelligent risks and explore new opportunities, ideas, and strategies. √

14. We understand our roles and are responsible and accountable for the performance of the profit center. √

Team Processes: Team Meeting Agreements

Agenda Field Support
Tuesday Morning Meeting

6:30 AM to 7:25 AM
Room 3193
Type of meeting
Facilitator:
Note Taker: Crew Change / Information Sharing

Agenda Topics
    A. Review Work Agreements for clarity and acknowledgments
    B. Technical Information Sharing
    C. Activity Recap
    D. PP&E - Performance Review
    E. Additional Agenda Items:

Team Processes: Peer-to-Peer Process & Agreements

Initially, the Facilities Reps developed the following principles for a Peer-to-Peer Process. Subsequently, the Field Support Team decided to adopt these principles for the entire team as an informal process (meaning no one was to be held accountable for doing these like on their PMP). The team intended to use these principles to improve overall team performance and team member interaction.

Guiding Principles:

1. **Defenselessness communication** - We want to be able to communicate about work situations without getting defensive ... so we can help each other solve / resolve problems. By so doing, we will improve our overall communication ability.

2. **Outside forces will not split us** - Whenever we have outside forces that have the potential to cause us problems (split us), we want to use the Peer-to-Peer Process to help us better understand each other's perspectives and learn how to prevent it next time.

3. **Tom** [their supervisor] **gets a consistent message from us** - We want Tom to get a consistent message from all of us. We also want him to see / believe we're achieving our potential. We intend to improve our working relationship with Tom.

4. **"Who better to talk to...?"** - We want to be able to talk to someone, like each other, who understands what we're up against.

5. **To learn timing and political correctness** - We want to use our discussions to determine on whom, and when, we can push back - like the business team, FMT's, etc. - without causing political and / or PMP problems for ourselves and our customers.

6. **Improve each other's working style** - We want to talk to each other and help each other improve our work styles versus trying to get others to change their style.

7. **Listen** - We want to really listen to each other... which doesn't mean we'll agree, but we won't let any disagreements get in the way of performing our jobs.

8. **Share information** - We intend to share the most appropriate information, realizing that schedules and work objectives get in the way sometimes. For example, it's important for people to attend our Tuesday meetings, but sometimes people can't come.

9. **We will not withhold** - If a teammate hears something about another teammate that's negative (or potentially negative), we'll bring it up to that person and / or the team as soon as appropriate. We intend to help that person and the team.

10. **The Peer-to-Peer is ours** - This process is to be used among ourselves, and it's not for PMP. However, we want it to help us improve in our PMP, avoiding any surprises that Tom might say to us - i.e., "so & so (OS) said ..."

11. **Talk to each other first** - If we have any problem amongst ourselves, we'll discuss it before others find out - especially Tom.

12. **It's an "inside job"** - We want to listen to understand versus listening to respond and judge each other. It's an inside job to notice we're getting defensive or judgmental. We're committed to "STOP" and really listen.

13. **Competitiveness is okay** - We encourage competitiveness, but it's not okay to try to make our light brighter by blowing out someone else's.

14. **We're proud to be a Field Support Team Member** - "I want to stop having to defend myself for being a member of the Field Support Team!"

Team Processes: Relationship Work Agreements

Agreement #1 Intention:

1. Each team member agrees to resolve or help resolve any / all team-related issues.

Conditions for acceptance / clarification:

A. It's our intention to be proactive with each other, to not let any issue go unresolved that would eventually cause problems, and to use this Agreement to improve team performance.

B. Whenever a team member has an issue to resolve, they will first go to others in private, and if they can't resolve it, then they will bring it up to the team.

C. Whenever two or more team members try to resolve an issue, each team member agrees 1) to listen to understand, 2) to swap roles and listen again 3) that no one will get defensive, 4) to express "what's needed," and 5) to resolve.

D. Resolving an issue means each team member will actively support team decisions and accurately represent those decisions to others.

E. We will not use words or body language that make the situation worse.

F. When we see a team member repeatedly breaking this Agreement, and it's a serious breach, we will: 1) address the problem in front of the group, 2) ask them what they feel is the problem, 3) as a group, explain what we feel is the problem, 4) try to resolve the problem, and 5) if we can't resolve, call in a mutually agreed-upon third party.

G. We'll watch our "zingers, joking, and cutting-up" with each other when there's a difficult or tense situation because it only makes things worse and hurts feelings.

H. If something is said and it hurts, "check it out" with them ASAP and resolve it.

I. If a team member needs to vent before they give another team member feedback or to resolve a conflict, it's okay to go to a third party, but it must remain confidential.

Agreement #2 Intention:

2. Each team member commits to support each other.

Conditions for acceptance/clarification:

A. We will review missed opportunities so we will not miss them again.
B. It's our intention to honor our commitment to each other so we can set the "standard" in CPDN.

Agreement #3 Intention:

3. Each team member will work to improve individual and team communications.

Conditions for acceptance/clarification:

A. We will communicate facts and clearly own when what we say could be opinions or assumptions.
B. We will listen to each other's opinions (and repeat it back) to make sure that we really hear each other. We intend to keep an open mind and to change our minds if appropriate.
C. If a team member checks it out with you, it's not about questioning that team member's commitment to the team. We just want to improve our one-on-one team communications.
D. We will not "badmouth" anyone, and we'll be open to feedback if others think we are.
E. When a team member experiences a problem, we'll own it, resolve it, and share the learnings with the team. We will not avoid or deny our role in it.

Team Processes: Team Performance Assessment Summary

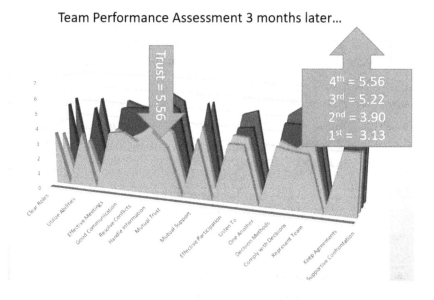

Team Performance Assessment 3 months later...

4th = 5.56
3rd = 5.22
2nd = 3.90
1st = 3.13

Trust = 5.56

This Team's Results / Benefits ... After 1 Year

Objective Measures New Income & Saved Surplus Material	$281,000
Subjective Measures 1,400 Labor Hours Saved	$70,000
Total Savings	$351,000
Team Building ROI	1,094%

Overall 45% Improvement

78% Increase - Trust

46% Increase – Mutual Support

61% Increase – Complying with Decisions

Example #3: International Project Team

Synopsis

Without strong internal processes and teammate trust, teams fall apart.

Such was the experience of Peter and Randy, co-project managers of an 85-person major capital project team. This team was responsible for designing and building a billion-dollar chemical plant.

Twenty-five teammates were from the client organization, which owned the plant. The other teammates were from an international engineering company. All 85 teammates were in the same office.

Team members constantly disagreed over work processes, and toxic interpersonal relationships caused additional stress and dysfunction.

First Workshop

After conducting teammate interviews, I learned many teammates had complaints about the number of required team meetings. They felt meetings were ineffective and not valuable.

We decided this was the issue to address in the first workshop. With support, the team created Work Agreements that mapped out how they would use agendas, identified desired outcomes, and laid ground rules to keep meetings on track. They also addressed how to speak up if a meeting went sideways.

After just one month of living their new Work Agreements, teammates reported they were getting more work done because they were not in so many meetings, and the meetings they did have were more productive, organized, and better facilitated.

The team declared the Work Agreements a success, and managers Randy and Peter estimated **they were able to save $10,000 a week in labor costs.**

Second & Third Workshops

This team wanted to move quickly. They scheduled their second workshop just three weeks after the first. In that workshop, they wanted to address team communications.

And just two weeks after that, they conducted their third workshop, where they addressed prioritizing work.

Here is a summary of their team conclusions. Below, you'll find their Team Business Plan with Work Agreements.

Summary of Team Recommendations

1. Meeting Behaviors: commit to living the Agreement below
2. Type of meeting & frequency changes [see below]
3. PDN: follow agreed upon process [by June 11 training]
4. Weekly reports: change to bi-weekly
5. Make realistic promises between PMT / Client
6. Improve Client Communications: follow agreement below
7. Roles & Responsibilities: clarify as needed
8. QII: First Things First philosophy: commit to live
9. Teammates agree to follow issued plans and procedures.

Teamwork Issue: Meetings
Teammates: Darlene, Troy, Ernest

The Problem is…
  a. There are too many valueless and unorganized (impromptu) meetings.
  b. Our meetings are not efficient or effective.
  c. There is lack of action item tracking and follow-through.
  d. There is a lack of consistent meeting notes and no decision register or action item register.

The Opportunity is …
  a. To reduce total meeting time and use that extra time toward achieving our schedule.
  b. To get more done in the meetings we attend – i.e., become more effective & efficient.
  c. To increase our team's performance in completing action items on time.

The Actions recommended are …
  1. **Ask all teammates to follow the letter and spirit of our Meeting Process Agreement** (see Agreement in next section)
     a. Steps to endorsement:
        i. Present this Agreement and meeting frequency changes to PMT for feedback, modification, and agreement.
        ii. After PMT and Advisory team agree, leads will roll out the Agreement to all teammates and ask for their endorsement.

2. **Clarify types of meetings and frequency**.
    a. Summary of "Meeting" Recommendations:
        i.   Reduce Morning Meeting to once per week; now called Weekly Meeting
        ii. Add Engineering Leads Meeting – conduct as needed
        iii. Capture Actions in IMS
        iv. BENEFIT: total time save is ~60+ man-hours per week

    b. **Weekly Meeting**
        i.   Frequency & length: Monday, 10–11AM
        ii. Owner: Cary
        iii. Purpose: Ensure all staff are aligned for the week ahead
        iv. Agenda: Cary will publish if deemed necessary
        v.   Scribe: Sara / PE will capture action items internal IMS, in real-time
        vi. Attendees: discipline lead, PMT, project engineers

    c. **Engineering "Issues" Meeting** - as-needed meeting
        i.   Frequency & Length: this will NOT BE A PANIC MEETING. You will be given no less than 24-hours' notice.
        ii. Purpose: address pressing, and common issues as needed
        iii. Owner: Linda
        iv. Scribe: Troy / other will capture action items internal IMS, in real-time
        v.   Attendees: if you are invited
        vi. Agenda: will accompany the notice

262 · DAN HOGAN

d. **PMT - as-needed meeting**
  i. Frequency & length: Every other Thursday 3:00 – 4:00 PM
  ii. Owner: Randy
  iii. Purpose: Discuss and clarify strategic issues such as task / role prioritization over the next 1-3 weeks
  iv. Agenda: Randy will publish if deemed necessary
  v. Scribe: Sara / PE will capture action items internal IMS, in real-time
  vi. Attendees: PMT

e. **PDN / Value Improvement capture**
  i. Frequency & Length: TBD - Tuesday 8:00 – 8:30AM
  ii. Owner: Linda
  iii. Scribe: Sara
  iv. Attendees: Project engineers, discipline leads, PMT
  v. Agenda: review last week's PDN

f. **Value Added Improvement Meeting**
  i. Frequency & length: TBD
  ii. Owner: Randy
  iii. Purpose: show clients how we add value
  iv. Agenda: TBD
  v. Scribe: Sara / PE will capture action items internal IMS, in real-time
  vi. Attendees: PMT

g. Procurement Meeting
  i. Frequency & length: TBD
  ii. Owner: Cary
  iii. Purpose: Ensure orders are placed on time
  iv. Agenda: TBD
  v. Scribe: Sara / PE will capture action items internal IMS, in real time
  vi. Attendees: PMT

h. Schedule Review Meetings
  i. Frequency & length: TBD
  ii. Owner: Randy
  iii. Purpose: Ensure PMT is making progress
  iv. Agenda: TBD
  v. Scribe: Sara / PE will capture action items internal IMS, in real time
  vi. Attendees: PMT

i. External Meetings
  i. We recommend IOU teammates use the Meeting Process Agreement in all external meetings.
  ii. We recommend that in the near future, when the PMT conducts an integrated team building workshop, the IOU presents this Agreement to the client and asks them if they would be willing to live by these practices.

Meeting Process Agreement

Team Choice:

1. Each teammate will do their part to ensure we have effective and efficient meetings.

Clarifications / Conditions for Acceptance:

A. All regularly scheduled meetings will have a clear purpose, clear outcomes, a realistic agenda distributed 24 hours in advance [identify preparation task], and the right people in attendance.
B. Regularly scheduled meetings will have a meeting owner who is responsible for facilitating and keeping the meeting on track. They will ensure proper meeting notes are taken and distributed.
C. Meeting closure: We will always restate our decision, understanding, and actions-owner-due-by-dates at the end of all meetings.
D. Action Items will be captured in IMS.
E. We agree to use the same level of efficiency and effectiveness in all informal meetings.
F. Everyone will make their thinking visible, even if it means expressing disagreement.
G. Meeting Ground Rules:
    - Show up on time, stay on task, and end on time.
    - "Let's take it outside." "Enough, let's move on."
    - Use the parking lot to capture important but not urgent ideas that will be addressed in future meetings or assigned to teammates to address.
    - Respectful and emotionally mature conversation.
    - None of us is as smart as all of us.
    - Come to a consensus even if you don't get everything you want.
    - Hold yourself and others accountable for living this Agreement.

Teamwork Issue: Communications

Teammates: Jackie, Tatiana, Johan, Michael

The Problem is...

a. There is disagreement as to what information needs to be documented and how.

b. The PDN process does not work effectively.

c. Some important information is withheld and / or not properly communicated from PMT to all teammates and vice versa.

d. There is no agreement as to when we need to use verbal or face-to-face communication as opposed to email or IMS.

e. There is a feeling of us versus them between engineering and PMT.

f. There is no agreed-upon way to express disagreement between teammates and leaders.

The Opportunity is...

a. To save time and to satisfy the client with a more effective PDN process.

b. To provide leaders and teammates with the right information at the right time.

c. To increase PMT and engineering collaboration.

d. To reduce misunderstandings and / or increase our likelihood of meeting the schedule because we are communicating properly, in emotionally mature ways.

The Actions recommended are...

1. **Create a behavioral Work Agreement** to address behavioral or interaction issues.

    a. The team will create the first draft (see below) and present it to the PMT for changes and eventual agreement.

    b. The teammates and the PMT leaders will cascade down this Agreement to all IOU teammates

2. **Improve client communication.**

    a. We recommend all teammates use the following "go bys" below to guide our client communications.

    b. We do this because there are times when verbal communications are sufficient and other times when communication needs to be documented.

    c. We recommend that our company provide more or additional training on how to use electronic project communications tools and software.

3. **Update weekly reports.**

    a. To add value and to save time, move to bi-weekly reports that are aligned with or sync with In-Control.

4. **Set realistic promises** between PMT and Client.
   a. Philosophy: Manage and adhere to the Quadrant II / First-Things-First model (see below).
   b. We recommend PMT first discuss deliverable due date promises with discipline leads before making promises to the client.
   c. If our discipline counterpart comes to you with last-minute requests, we will be firm. We can't accept last minute requests all the time. We don't want to accept bad planning on their part.
   d. We recommend all these because:
      i. It will help mitigate us vs. them (engineering vs. PMT).
      ii. It will help mitigate last-minute "drop stuff on my desk" incidents.
   e. We all agreed to the above.

5. **Clarify the IOU PDN process**.
   a. Leaders have discussed and agreed on the internal PDN process. The process will be vetted with the Client and then rolled out to all to follow.

Communications Agreement

Team Choice:
Each team member will communicate their thoughts and feelings in an emotionally mature and professional way.

Clarifications / Conditions for Acceptance:
A. We follow the spirit & intent of our One Way Values.
B. Emotional and professional mature communication can be described as tone of voice, word choice, body language, assertive versus aggressive, etc.
C. When we notice disagreement or tension in a conversation, we will stop and define terms or facts. We also commit to using the What to Say statements.
D. If we feel or believe another is being inappropriate, we will remind them of this Communications Agreement.
E. We also agree to give positive reinforcement to our teammates when we see or hear effective communication.
F. Not only do we agree to hold ourselves accountable, but we will also hold others accountable in a safe and supportive way, and that means we will speak up and not keep silent.
G. We don't condone behind-the-back negative conversation. We advocate that all teammates discuss their frustrations and resolve them.
H. If a team member continues to break any of our team Work Agreements, we will escalate this issue to a higher authority.

What to Say

Use these statements to advocate, inquire, or resolve conflict on any team.

Improved Advocacy
- Here's what I'm thinking and how I got there…
- Some of the assumptions I've made are…..

Improved Inquiry
- What data are you using to reach that conclusion…?
- What's leading you to make that conclusion…?

When You Disagree
- Tell me again how you came to believe this point of view.
- Are you using any data that I may not have considered?
- Am I understanding you correctly that you're saying…?

Dealing with an Impasse
- What do we know for a fact?
    - What do we think is true but don't have any data for yet?
    - Are there things we don't know?
    - What is unknowable?
- It seems / feels like we're at an impasse. Do you have ideas that might help us come to a new Work Agreement?

Teamwork Issue: Prioritize Work, Tasks, Packages
Teammates: Sumiti, Lora, Linda, Sharon

The Problem is...
- a. There are too many last-minute requests that cause panic.
- b. There are too many unrealistic requests / deadlines.
- c. Too often teammates are not aware of and / or don't follow established procedures.

The Opportunity is...
- a. To save time by reducing last-minute crisis situations and by being more flexible.
- b. To increase our internal collaboration, plus our collaboration with our customers.
- c. To create alignment between all IOU teammates and leaders as to what is realistic.

Statements of Fact...
- a. When the Service Order is signed, and the schedule is published, prioritization will help.
- b. Until the reorganization and alignments are published, there will be uncertainty in people's minds as to our priorities.
- c. We believe that living the other sub-team Agreements will help resolve the "prioritization" issue.

The Actions recommended are...

1. **Adopt / agree to live by First-Things-First.**

     a. Ask all PMT leaders and leads to abide by the QII First-Things-First philosophy (see next section) and adopt it as an individual responsibility.

2. **Ask teammates to do the following.**

     a. If you believe you and your direct project supervisor are not aligned with respect to your work task prioritization, stop immediately to talk about it and resolve it.

     b. If you are asked by your direct project supervisor to stop what you are doing and do something else, seek to understand why. Maybe it is not really a crisis. However, if you go forward with the new task, be certain to negotiate and agree on what you will and will not do.

3. **Ask all teammates to follow the issued plans and procedures.**

     a. When gaps or misunderstandings are discovered, use accepted Client and Engineering Company procedures.

272 · DAN HOGAN

First Things First: A Time Management Philosophy

	Urgent	Not Urgent
Important	QI: Crisis, panic, pressing problems, missed deadlines, "fires" you have to address now	**QII:** Proper / realistic planning, crisis prevention, building positive relationships, having enough time to complete deliverables **Say YES!**
Not Important	QIII: Interruptions: hallway talk, last-minute requests for info Say No…	QIV: Low value or duplicate work Say No…
	Time	

Teamwork Issue: Roles & Responsibilities

Teammates: Sara, Carlos, Guillermo

The Problem is...

a. There is misalignment on roles and responsibilities in some areas.

b. There is confusion and lack of understanding of PMT roles and responsibilities.

c. Too often teammates don't feel empowered or engaged.

d. There is a feeling of us versus them between engineering and PMT.

The Opportunity is...

a. To improve effectiveness and efficiency by having a greater number of teammates and leaders aligned on roles and responsibilities.

b. To increase the likelihood of meeting the schedule because a greater number of teammates and leaders are following through on their roles and responsibilities.

c. To increase PMT and engineering collaboration.

d. To increase trust, accountability, and collaboration throughout the project team.

Statements of Fact...

a. We believe that living the other sub-team Agreements will help resolve the "prioritization" issue.

The Actions recommended are...

1. Realize we are currently in a re-alignment with our client.
   a. Some of the role ambiguity could be mitigated in the new alignment.

2. Empower individual teammates through growth.
   a. Growing individual capability is important. Therefore, we recommend PMT, and department leads do more to empower individual teammates to help them grow and develop.

3. Speak up if not in agreement.
   a. If any teammate or leader believes they are not in agreement with respect to their roles, responsibility, and duties, they have PMT's permission to speak to their direct supervisor.
   b. Follow these steps:
      i. Review your roles as listed in the PEP.
      ii. Identify any changes you'd like to make such as where you believe you should have more empowerment.
      iii. Discuss with your direct project supervisor.
      iv. Come to an agreement.
      v. If you can't come to an agreement, team leaders will make the decision.

4. Optional: Clarify roles through group activity.
   a. If deemed of value, use the following roles exercise.
   b. Consider a lunch-and-learn where all key roles are presented and clarified.

Roles & Responsibilities Team-Building Workshop Agenda

Desired Outcome: Discuss, clarify, confirm, and agree on who does what, when, and how.

Time Commitment: 2-4 hours
Participants: 7 teammates

Agenda
A. Kick-off
B. Agree on the Desired Outcome
C. Agree to believe and behave as one unified team
D. RMT's Role Clarification exercise
- One person at a time gives answers to the questions.
- Dialogue follows.
- Time permitting, create new Work Agreements & teammate understandings
- Capture conclusions in the Team Business Plan.
- If you run out of time, complete as many possible, then schedule a second session to continue.
E. Close

Example #4: Architectural Design Company

Synopsis

This is the story of an architectural design firm with over 100 employees. Leroy, the partner-in-charge, asked, "Can you facilitate one of those off-site meetings you do?"

I told him I'd be happy to. "What do you want to accomplish?" I asked.

He said he wanted to increase trust and to get the other founding partner to change his work behavior. The partner was driving everyone crazy. He was making customers angry. He was even running off some of their best employees.

My prospective client wanted his partner to stop all the whining and complaining. The company was having its best year ever, and he didn't want to blow it!

After I interviewed all the other partners and principles, I validated the head partner's perception. There was a lack of trust. The other leaders were also very frustrated with the other founding partner. Most believed that if he were gone, their problems would be solved.

I learned in the interviews that the organization had very little team and organizational structure. They had no strategic plan and no team operating system. Everyone agreed they needed a vision and more structure.

I reported back to the head partner and reflected what I was seeing.

I said, "Sometimes, the best way to address dysfunctional behavior is first to resolve work process issues. I recommend that in the offsite meeting, we create the organization's first strategic plan and operating structure. Once that is in place if a particular leader or partner doesn't do their part, then you can easily implement corrective action or termination."

He agreed to that plan.

First Workshop

In the first workshop, the team created five strategies, along with several process and behavioral Work Agreements. They even took the time to clarify roles and responsibilities.

They also agreed I would facilitate their leadership team meetings as part of the improvement process.

Second & Third Workshop

In place of additional formalized workshops, I facilitated the team's biweekly leadership team meetings for the next six months.

During our time together, we made our way through every one of Right-Minded Teamwork's 5 Elements. Below is their Team Business Plan.

Note: This final example has been abbreviated down to the essentials since there are already two preceding Team Business Plan examples, which include full details.

ABC Architectural Design Firm

Mission Statement

To provide quality architecture through personal service that responds to our clients' needs while providing a vibrant, positive environment for our employees.

Summary of Strategic Goals

Strategic Goal 1:
Deliver Exceptional Architectural Design & Service (details below)

Strategic Goal 2:
Be an Awesome Place to Work (details below)

Strategic Goal 3:
Increase Financial Value of Firm

Strategic Goal 4:
Expand Present Markets & Capture New Ones

Strategic Goal 5:
Contribute to Our Community

Strategic Goals

Strategic Goal 1: Deliver Exceptional Architectural Design & Service

Sponsor: Marc

Important Perspectives:
- Clients & prospective clients
- Suppliers / JVs / Contractors
- Community – a sense of pride in ABC's work
- ABC's employees – a sense of pride

Focus:
- Quality, innovation, TQM service to clients
- Creating a learning organization
- Vertical Studio work-process efficiency
- Efficient, competent, talented, and productive employees

ACTIONS

1.1: Create, implement, and follow an Exceptional Design Standard that will ensure we raise the bar on the level of our design.
  a. Describe & define the "exceptional" service standard.
  b. Train employees in 1) the ABC Exceptional Service Standard, and 2) capture specific service standards for each employee in their individual performance plans.
  c. Create and implement a client satisfaction "exceptional service" scorecard process to understand how ABC is doing and identify needed areas for improvement.

1.2   Maintain a continuous-improvement, total-quality process in all phases and levels at ABC.

Proposal & Contract Stage

a. Improve the entire proposal-to-contract process so both clients and ABC employees have a positive experience while creating clear deliverables, timelines, accountabilities, and other quality and service expectations.

Presentation Stage

a. Improve ABC's marketing presentation capability.

Job Stage

a. Fully implement the Vertical Team process.
b. Fully implement the QA / QC process.
c. Implement a web-based project management site for design and construction.

Follow-up Stage

a. Consistently follow-up on projects.

Strategic Goal 2: Be an Awesome Place to Work

Sponsor: Bob

Important Perspectives:
- Employees
- ABC management
- Clients / Suppliers / Industry

Focus:
- Just and fair rewards, benefits, and compensation
- Retention / turnover / recruitment
- Happy / satisfied employees
- The right people, with the right skills, in the right jobs, at the right time

ACTIONS

2.1: Ensure the right people with the right skills are in the right job at the right time and are delivering "exceptional architectural service."

    a. Create an awesome, effective, unified leadership team that is fun to work with.

    b. Establish and implement a partner peer review system using a Leadership 360 upward appraisal system.

    c. Agree on Associate's roles, and accountabilities.

2.2: Create an awesome, can-do, positive ABC culture and physical environment.

    a. Create and implement an annual, confidential employee perception survey (conduct two surveys in the first 12 months, then annually thereafter).

    b. Ensure the Employee Performance Review system is indeed helping the firm 1) have the right people with the right skills and 2) meet or exceed ABC's five Strategic Goals.

2.3: Develop and implement a standardized, flexible interviewing / hiring process using behavioral-based concepts, candidate accomplishments, and ABC's Strategic Goals.

    a. Develop minimum competency hiring standards for key positions.

2.4: Develop a leadership / employee training and development strategy that directly links to ABC's five Strategic Goals.

    a. Leadership: Using the leader upward appraisal / individual improvement plan, the firm will support / fund the leader to attend training to improve leadership skills.

    b. Employee: Using the individual performance reviews and the (potential) employee survey to identify needed training, the firm will support / fund training and development courses for employees.

    c. Improve communication of office procedures, standards, and policies.

2.5: Ensure ABC has a just and fair rewards and compensation system.

    a. Assess the current formal and informal compensation system that will help ABC meet or exceed its Strategic Goals.

2.6: Celebrate our company, team, and individual successes.

    a. Create ways to celebrate with our clients, suppliers, and employees.

Sample Roles & Responsibilities

Example 1: Leroy

What do I contribute to the firm?
- Leadership through final decision-making when required to resolve issues
- Personal and professional presence in the community through volunteer organizations and political activities
- Primary networking, public relations, and project procurement effort
- Provide the glue to hold the organization stable

What authority do I currently have?
- President and chairman of the board of directors
- Own majority of voting stock
- Can make final decisions (only with the majority of board vote)

What do I need?
- Need no further authority and feel no boundaries within the framework of what we all agree to as the best interest of the firm

Leroy: What Will I...

START

1. Be more organized: delegate direct project-related issues, solicit feedback regularly from principals, receive feedback from principals regarding when I am being impulsive
2. Push/direct people back to solving own interpersonal relationships
3. Spend more time with employees, getting to know them – dedicating the time to personally interact and recognize contributors
4. Trust all principals in their judgment and level of interest – demonstrate support when delegating, self-monitor behaviors when delegating, forgive the failures, negotiate timelines and expectations, receive, and listen and positively respond to push back from Principles
5. Share more of the public image of the firm – communicate when events "expect" attendance and when they "may" attend – ask for what is needed, and discuss with Mark to determine in Monday management meeting; ask people to go to events "with me"
6. Be more patient with employees and Principals – ask for feedback and coaching; increase self-awareness of body language and tone of voice
7. Recognize that everyone doesn't think and make decisions like me – raise self-awareness, self-monitor reactions to different styles, rely on trust

STOP

1. 1Being stressed out by daily situations – focus on the "start," delegate project-specific issues, personally commit to making the mental shift; double-check when delegating actions
2. Being impatient – (see above)
3. Working 12-hour days – schedule a vacation; make the mental shift that it won't end if I give responsibility away
4. Letting the activities and demands of our clients control my life – reprioritize events and communicate priorities to peers

CONTINUE

1. To provide leadership and vision for the firm
2. Mentor those I feel have the ability and drive to succeed
3. Make the firm financially successful by obtaining high-profit projects
4. Take the image of the firm to the highest level possible
5. Follow my plan to dispose of my stock in the firm and retire

Example 2: Bob

What do I contribute to the firm?

- A liaison in computer technology between users and non-users of CAD (because I took it upon myself to understand the system and its implications)
- Heavily involved in staffing human resource functions
- Agent of change for policies that beg to be implemented because they have been successfully used by other companies whose growth rates have similarly demanded change
- The implementer of solutions that are necessary to achieve the goals and vision of the company
- Represent this firm as one of its leaders

What authority do I currently have?

- Review and make recommendations for software and equipment purchases related to CAD
- Suggest alternatives in our policies and decisions
- PIC lead committee member for human resources
- Draft proposals for projects and give input to others when asked

What do I need?

- Receive input and increase staff before a crisis occurs
- Change the culture in ways beneficial to the firm
- Support of all other Principles in enhancing our image through understanding and dedication to quality programs and policies

ABC Architectural Design Process Work Agreements

1. Each Principle will either print their own budget reports OR provide a list of job numbers to their accounting contact person to get the budget reports.
    *   Schedule time with the Project Manager to discuss budget and completion reports.
    *   Create a plan of action; ensure that the Project Manager understands where they are on the project and what needs to happen to ensure a quality project is delivered within budget and on time.
    *   PIC meets with PMs twice per month.

2. "Design people" (Leroy, Mark, Marc, Cheryl) will meet together to decide what to do with controversial designs during the proposal phase.
    *   What can we do within the budget?
    *   How much are we willing to invest of ABC's money?
    *   Do we go back to the client & sell the design to get more money?
    *   If it is determined that the project will require an ABC investment, present to Management Team for: Approval Veto, Alternative solutions

The team also made two additional process Agreements two weeks later:

3. Print and establish a list of PIC, PM to input into the Win2 system.
   a. Ensure Ralph checks the list for accuracy.

4. We agree that if we cannot accomplish the outcomes & accountabilities, we agreed to, we will raise the issue with Principles to re-evaluate & prioritize

And, after another four weeks, the team added another three process Agreements:

5. Discuss Aged Receivables at the last Management Meeting each month.
   a. Accounting to provide Aged Receivables to Stephanie by Wednesday prior to distribution and review.
   b. Each Principle agrees to review the Aged Receivables Report prior to the Management Meeting.
6. A report will not be labeled "final" until an assessment of the accounting system has been made and agreement by Management Team has been reached regarding how the "profitability" of a project is reported.

7. Every two weeks in our Management Meeting, we will discuss Forecast Staffing Needs (at the end of the meeting).
   a. We agree that Ralph should be present for this portion of the meeting.
   b. Leroy should share any relevant information early on and is excused from this portion of the meeting.

Architectural Design Action Work Agreements

Intention:

1. When we discuss and agree on our individual roles and responsibilities, we will be open and honest (in a business context); we will address the issue and not attack the person.

Conditions for Acceptance / Clarifications:

- None were made for this Agreement.

Intention:

2. Each team member agrees to address issues without getting defensive.

Conditions for Acceptance / Clarifications:

A. If someone does get defensive, it's okay if we acknowledge it, quickly apologize for it, and move on.

B. It's not about being perfect. It's about recovery and rebounding.

C. If someone does get defensive, we will:

- Reframe the issue
- Ask, "Are you feeling defensive…?"
- Say, "I'm sorry, but I don't think you understand my point…will you reflect back to me what you're hearing me say?"

Intention:

3. We will discuss and agree to upfront on the ABC direction we are going, and we will all visibly support that decision.

Conditions for Acceptance / Clarifications:

    A. If we feel a Principal has not upheld this Agreement, we will bring it up with that Principal and remind them of this Agreement. We will provide behavior-specific and / or specific examples of instances when we perceived this Agreement was not being upheld. We will resolve the issue.

    B. Our intention for this Agreement is to be unified outside this room, and when we have disunity, we work it out in this room.

Intention:

4. We will address each other one-on-one when there is a difficult issue with the intent to resolve and reach an agreement.

Conditions for Acceptance / Clarifications:

    A. If we cannot reach an agreement, we will raise difficult issues in a group setting with the intent to reach an agreement. We will not engage inside conversations with the intent of avoiding or politicking.

Intention:

5. If a Principal feels that they are overloaded and cannot perform all the tasks or meet all the expectations, they will call it out at the Management Meeting.

Conditions for Acceptance / Clarifications:

   A. If we perceive a Principal is overloaded and is not meeting expectations, we will call it out.
   B. Our intention for this Agreement is to create the right work workload balance to meet our Strategic Plan.
   C. Whenever possible, we will educate / inform each other on our current workload (increase understanding of what is on each other's plate) so that we improve our work efficiencies, like reducing callbacks.

Intention:

6. We will not engage in negative discussions about another Principal.

Conditions for Acceptance / Clarifications:

   A. If a Principal speaks negatively about another, we will stop them and encourage them to work that issue out with that Principal.
   B. We will provide assistance and guidance in helping each other go back to the source and reach an agreement.

The End

On behalf of **Reason** and all the **Right-Minded Teammate Decision-Makers and Team Facilitators**, we extend our best wishes to you and your teammates as you create another *Right-Minded Team that Works Together as One*.

CPSIA information can be obtained
at www.ICGtesting.com
Printed in the USA
BVHW092130270322
632588BV00002B/19